MW01505042

LOVE

THE GREATEST GIFT

A Journey of Unconditional Love Based on God's Original Design

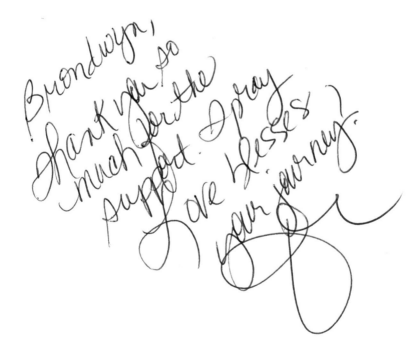

Brondwyn,

Thank you so much for the support. I pray Love blesses your journey.

LOVE
THE GREATEST GIFT

A Journey of Unconditional Love Based on God's Original Design

JACQUELINE CAMPHOR

ACCENTUALS
CONSULTING
HOUSTON

LOVE: THE GREATEST GIFT

Published by Accentuals Consulting, LLC
1700 Post Oak Boulevard, Suite 600
Houston, TX, 77056 USA
http://accentualsco.com

© 2015 by Jacqueline Camphor

All rights reserved. No part of this publication may be reproduced, stored in a retrieval system, or transmitted, in any form or by any means—electronic, mechanical, photocopying, recording, or otherwise—without the prior written permission of the author or publisher. For all e-book versions, including but not limited to Kindle, Nook, or PDF, this e-book may not be resold or given away to others.

The literary references recommended throughout this book are offered as a resource to you. These references are not intended in any way to be or imply an endorsement on the part of Accentuals Consulting, LLC, nor do we vouch for their content.

All the stories in this book are true, but most of the names have been changed to protect the privacy of the people mentioned. Permission has been obtained for usage of all other personal accounts.

Unless otherwise noted, all scripture quotations are taken from the Holy Bible (New International Version), copyright 1973, 1978, 1984 by International Bible Society. Used by permission of Zondervan Publishing House. All rights reserved. Scripture quotations identified as "KJV" are taken from the Holy Bible (King James Version), copyright 2010 by Holman Bible Publishers. All rights reserved. Scripture quotations identified as "ESV" are taken from the Holy Bible (English Standard Version), copyright 2001 by Crossway Bibles, a publishing ministry of Good News Publishers. All rights reserved.

ISBN 978-0-9965739-1-7
eISBN 978-0-9965739-0-0
ISBN: 0996573917
Cover design by Andi Saleh
Cover (front) photo by Laila Juliana
Cover (back) photo by Emile C. Browne
Library of Congress Control Number: 2015912262

Printed in the United States of America

~ For the One who first loved me ~

ACKNOWLEDGMENTS

My God, you never cease to amaze me. Your patience and love are timeless. Thank you for how you show up in my everyday just to let me know you're always near. Thank you for choosing me for this mission. We did it! I pray this work reaches the hearts and souls of those who need to know and experience your forever love.

My beloved parents, I am eternally grateful for all you are and all you do for me and our family. Next to God, there is no greater love than your own.

My brother, Chris, you inspire me on so many levels. Thank you for always supporting my dreams and having a godly word of encouragement to share.

My bestie and sister, Tasha Johnson, thank you for the many years of selfless love and friendship without conditions. You are the best ride-or-die; it's been a fun-loving adventure.

My cousins, like brothers and best friends, Bryon Diltz and Travis Diltz, thank you for always being there. I am blessed beyond measure to have you in my life. You keep me lifted.

My heroes, the brave of heart (Ciarra McClinton, Nicole Mosely, Tara Camp, Edgar and Jacqueline Hardy, Jessica Johnson, and the many others), who so boldly shared your stories for this mission, thank you a million times over. Your transparency is a blessed gift, and I pray God will use your courage for healing and restoration to a hurting and dying world.

My global visibility coach extraordinaire, Nikki Woods, thank you for your expert advisement and accountability through this entire process. I have learned so much from you and appreciate your helping take me to new levels in my journey.

My team at EBM Professional Services, Michelle Chester and Elaine Garcia, as well as CreateSpace, I couldn't have finished well without your keen eye to detail. Thank you for making the editorial process an enlightening and pleasurable one.

A Reader's Perspective, Nakia Laushaul, thank you for rocking it out with the book formatting and being so efficient. You are truly a Godsend.

My family and friends, who have invested in my life in so many respects and allowed me to go under to finish this work, I thank you. You are sincerely the *why* in my journey, and your continued love and support help me live out my purpose.

CONTENTS

My Story 13

The Greatest Love of All 19

What Love Is Not 25

Chapter 1: Love Does Not Envy.....................................27

Chapter 2: Love Does Not Boast.....................................33

Chapter 3: Love Is Not Proud 39

Chapter 4: Love Is Not Rude...44

Chapter 5: Love Is Not Self-Seeking 50

Chapter 6: Love Is Not Easily Angered 54

Chapter 7: Love Keeps No Record of Wrongs 58

Chapter 8: Love Does Not Delight in Evil.......................62

What Love Is...71

Chapter 9: Love Is Patient...73

Chapter 10: Love Is Kind 78

Chapter 11: Love Rejoices With the Truth 83

Chapter 12: Love Always Protects 87

Chapter 13: Love Always Trusts......................................93

Chapter 14: Love Always Hopes 99

Chapter 15: Love Always Perseveres..................................104

Learning to Love...109

Chapter 16: Loving God...111

Chapter 17: Loving Self...122

Chapter 18: Loving Through Courtship..........................130

Chapter 19: Loving Your Spouse.....................................143

Chapter 20: Loving Your Children...................................157

Chapter 21: Loving Your Blended Family.......................169

Chapter 22: Loving Your Parents.....................................177

Chapter 23: Loving Thy Neighbor...................................187

Chapter 24: Loving Your Enemies...................................195

Chapter 25: Loving After a Loss......................................204

Chapter 26: Love Never Fails...212

My Story 2.0..219

Resources...229

AND now I will show you the most excellent way. If I speak in the tongues of men or of angels, but do not have love, I am only a resounding gong or a clanging cymbal. If I have the gift of prophecy and can fathom all mysteries and all knowledge, and if I have a faith that can move mountains, but do not have love, I am nothing. If I give all I possess to the poor and surrender my body to the flames, but have not love, I gain nothing. Love is patient, love is kind. It does not envy, it does not boast, it is not proud. It is not rude, it is not self-seeking, it is not easily angered, it keeps no record of wrongs. Love does not delight in evil but rejoices with the truth. It always protects, always trusts, always hopes, always perseveres. Love never fails. But where there are prophecies, they will cease; where there are tongues, they will be stilled; where there is knowledge, it will pass away. For we know in part and we prophesy in part, but when perfection comes, the imperfect disappears. When I was a child, I talked like a child, I thought like a child, I reasoned like a child. When I became a man, I put the childish ways behind me. Now we see but a poor reflection as in a mirror; then we shall see face to face. Now I know in part; then I shall know fully, even as I am fully known. And now these three remain: faith, hope, and love. But the greatest of these is love.

1 Corinthians 12:31–13:13 (NIV)

MY STORY

You know my name, not my story. You see
my smile, not my pain. -Unknown

I T HAD BEEN ONE OF THE MOST PAINFUL SEASONS OF
my life. At age forty, my life was not even close to what I had imagined it would be. I had spent so much of my life's journey looking out
for and trying to take care of everyone else that I had nothing left to
give myself. Albeit, I was a strong, passionate woman of faith who
had loved hard and given generously. God had blessed me beyond
measure in so many respects of my life, yet the one thing I wanted
most of all was that unimaginable, unconditional love from a good,
godly husband and the incomparable gift of being a mother. Sure, I
had a wealth of family and friends who enveloped me with love and
inspiration, but that one BIG thing was missing for me: a family of
my own.

I had traveled the world to some of the most amazing places and
experienced many of the wonders of this world and its unique cultures. I had consistently given back in service to my church, local
community, and abroad. I had cared for and mentored kids of all

ages, from volunteering in the newborn nursery at the hospital to teaching teens life skills. I was always on my grind but never married to a career. I had started my own consulting practice where I had flexibility for whatever kind of work-life balance I desired. Even still, during this season of my life, I was empty and broken. By this time, I figured I would have been married to the man of my dreams with a tribe of mini "us." I had spent my entire adult life dating, and I had met every kind of man, it seemed. Yet, in terms of a relationship, here I was starting all over again.

Some of the men I dated were loving and supportive, while others were abrasive. There were the brief dating interests and those where we had both overstayed our welcome. I had dated men who were unavailable, and the more I did, there were pieces of me that also became unavailable. There were men who later claimed they just weren't ready, and there were those who had made promises but after getting attached, it became clear there were no intentions of fulfilling those promises; it was just a selfish attempt to keep me around—for what, I'm not sure. Then there were those who were really great guys but just not *my* great guy.

I would often get questions on dates asking what my story was or comments about how they couldn't believe a woman as wonderful as myself was still single. I would even get the "You must be crazy!" comments because they believed something must be wrong with a woman if she hadn't gotten married or had kids by a certain age. So many were trying to figure out what was up with me, and trust me, some days so was I, as the common denominator in all of my relationships *was me*. After a while, I think even I was starting to believe the lie that something indeed must be wrong with me…what other reason could there be? Some would ask, "Are your standards too high?" Having to answer that question was disheartening because I knew the answer was no…and quite the opposite of high. When I looked at my past, I saw a woman who chose to settle. I suppose I chose to settle because, deep down inside, I believed that what I really wanted didn't actually exist or was too far from my reach.

All around me, dating and married couples were turning in their commitment cards because someone in the relationship didn't meet the other's needs on some level; so I had unconsciously learned to hardly ever rock the boat in my relationships, was always "nice," and shied away from confrontation. I, too, had bought into the world's idea of relationships and not the design that God truly intended for each of us. I had been a woman who was committed to one man at a time. The person I am didn't know how to do it any other way; doing anything other than that just felt dishonest to me—it felt wrong. However, I had become enslaved to this conundrum we call dating and accepted it, as so many others had, as status quo. I kept encountering countless men who wanted the benefits of having a relationship but not the responsibility of commitment. So, the world's outlook was very confusing to me.

In those moments, I found myself wanting to retreat to my college years when relationships were much more simple and promising. I was just worn out from "the game." It seemed like finding that good and perfect match for myself was just nowhere in view until him. As I was turning the corner of the last leg of my thirty-ninth year already injured, without notice, this amazing man showed up in my life. It seemed as if I had finally met *the one*. After all the never-ending years of dating, sadly, this was the first time I had ever really been courted. To me, he was a beautiful surprise. He was handsome, a gentleman, and did everything for me with love and class. I had waited my whole life for a man like him. It was refreshing yet foreign to me all at the same time. In a lot of ways, I don't think I truly knew how to receive him because it had been so long since I had met someone so genuine; I just simply wasn't use to someone like him. He held my hand like he never wanted to let it go. The way he loved me was a blessing. How could I not have fallen for him? He had promised me the world, and I found myself doing things I had never done in any other relationship and opening up in ways I never imagined.

There were lots of firsts for me in that relationship: the first time I had proactively called my parents and family about the man in my life; the first time I had introduced him to key people who meant the world to me; and the first time I had really loved a man to an unconditional point. We had started planning a future together with all of the joys I had always envisioned. We both were in awe of each other, and I was the happiest I had ever been. When that relationship suddenly ended, my heart was shattered. I blamed myself for why things concluded with us. I thought if what I believed I had with him was true and it didn't end in marriage, maybe my view of love was distorted, or my perception of love was warped. He and I had drummed up this imagery of our lives for the rest our lives, and I had sold myself to our vision. I had come to the conclusion and was sure that it was him that I was supposed to spend the rest of my life with; I was so sure I was willing to make the compromises even on the things that really mattered to me all because I believed he was enough. I fought God for my plans to take precedence, even though He kept quietly urging me to give my plans to Him. Nonetheless, there wasn't a day that went by that I didn't think about him.

For days, I prayed and hoped that we would find that place back together where things were once so beautiful and hopeful. But the days grew into weeks; the weeks grew into months. I cried many days. I fought to stay strong. I reached out to a close friend for solace, but there was a part of me that didn't want to burden anyone with my pain. So I kept a smile on my face and my head held high, but behind the smile I was dying inside. I questioned why God would allow me to experience such a blessing yet remove the one thing that meant more to me than anything. I asked God, *Why me?* Why now after having waited for so long for the very thing I had prayed for consistently. For in that moment, it felt like a cruel joke. Although I had been blessed in so many areas of my life, I would have traded it all for that one thing I always desired: real love.

I wanted to believe love was possible for me, but after everything I had been through, I wasn't so sure anymore. I was tired of all the brokenness…all the dead ends. I'd had enough of the letdowns. So, I had gotten good with hiding my pain. I had found things to occupy my mind and my time. But after some time, the hiding got exhausting and began to wear me down. Then one August afternoon, I found myself numb at first, and then the floodgates opened in my eyes, and I began to pour out all that had hurt me. Over and over again, I was told by so many how amazing I was. I had guys whom I didn't share an interest with trying to lock me down. But at that moment, my heart was far from any of those guys, as I was fighting to keep pushing my life forward. As I began to try weeding out the casual from the serious, I'm sure I had left some scars along the way, yet not intentionally.

I asked God what my reason for being here was…what was it He wanted from me, as I felt I had given of myself to so many every day, yet it seemed I had absolutely nothing left to give, nothing left for Him or anyone else. What in my life was worth the living, I asked. I wanted so badly to hear God's voice, and then I received a call from a relative who answered: "God needs you because if you fall, so many others will fall with you; you keep so many of us lifted." I had no idea and was humbled by his words. As that late summer afternoon progressed, the tears began to dry, and this strength began to grow inside me like nothing I had ever experienced before. Although I didn't fully understand why the month of new beginnings felt like it was a month of endings, I chose to trust God. And I wasn't going to let the enemy beat me down with thoughts of defeat, but I was going to win by walking in faith when nothing seemed like it was going right in that area of my life. I decided not to go out that evening and instead get some much-needed rest, as I was going to need myself in the morning; I had to be ready for what God was about to do…

THE GREATEST LOVE OF ALL

For God so loved the world that He gave
His one and only son. -John 3:16

YOU CAN SEARCH YOUR WHOLE LIFE FOR LOVE—REAL, lasting, unimaginable, unconditional love—and miss it entirely. Women have given their bodies over to degrading self-images and willful sex in hopes of winning a man's heart or securing the leading role of love in a man's life. Men have practically sold their self-respect and/or spent their entire inheritance trying to win the love and affection of a woman. People do self-destructive things in the name of love. Yet, there is only One who can give love at the highest capacity you'll ever know or experience in this life. If you have never known or experienced this kind of love, clearly you have not met the Author and Creator of love. Please, let me introduce you. His name is Jesus, and love is He. God is love. His love is free for everyone and available to you for the receiving. There is no greater love you'll ever know than the love of His own.

Why God chose me to love, why He loves me so much, I don't think I'll ever fully know, but I know I don't want Him to ever stop. I am overwhelmingly grateful He loves me the way He does. I get amazed without ceasing by His goodness. Even as long and as much as my parents and family have known me, there is still no one who knows me more than He does. I know I can trust Him. He has my best interest at heart even when, on the surface, it doesn't appear that way. He's the best provider, a caring confidant, an enthusiastic encourager, a constant covering, a wise leader—the list of attributes is incessant. When I'm hard on myself, He gives me mercy. When I'm not feeling like I deserve His love, He gives me grace. No matter how many times I feel like I've failed Him, He's still courtside cheering me on for the win.

He's there for you, too. God loves you just as much, if not more. He loves you to such a degree that nothing you have ever done nor will ever do is beyond repair or separates you from His love. His love for you is so boundless that it is estimated that between AD 30 and 33, the Creator of the world gave His *one and only* son to be crucified for the sins of this world...your sins. God loves what He created (you and I) with such fervor that He gave the very essence of who He is and all He created you to be for you to have the chance to choose a life eternally with Him. He has demonstrated to us what love is by giving what He loved the most: a manifestation of Himself—His Mini-Me.

The greatest gift you will ever receive has been modeled by the unconditional giving of Himself. Have you ever loved someone so much that no matter how many mistakes he or she made, how many times he or she accepted less than what was best for himself or herself, or how many times he or she rejected you or your encouraging words you still loved that person and prayed for God's best in his or her life? Well, that's the kind of love God has for you! It doesn't matter how many times you've fallen or how much perceived defeat you've faced, He still wants you to experience the most amazing life of unconceivable love...His kind of love.

In His greatest demonstration of love, God illustrated three very important things: He chose; He gave; and He redeemed—all action and all without conditions. Nothing about His love is based on empty words or mere feelings. His love was designed to be permanent and not a temporary assignment. His love was intended for your good, not harm. Let's explore that further.

He Chose

Love is a choice. We know love as a result of God exhibiting it to us through His choosing of us. He chose you when He formed you in your mother's womb: "Your eyes saw my unformed body. All the days ordained for me were written in your book before one of them came to be" (Psalm 139:16). When He gave you your first breath, He made a commitment to you for eternity.

Jameis Winston was selected by the Tampa Bay Buccaneers as the number one pick for the 2015 National Football League (NFL) Draft after completing his sophomore year of college at Florida State University. His performance as a star quarterback is bar none. His list of accolades is unending, from being named the youngest Heisman Trophy winner to the Offensive MVP of the 2014 BCS National Championship Game against Auburn. Yet, amid all of the accomplishments and stardom, Jameis has been in the headlines with numerous scandals—allegations of sexual assault, shoplifting, and other public complaints. Even with a troubled past, Tampa Bay chose to see something extraordinary in Jameis. Like Jameis, we all have scandals in our headlines. Whether we told ourselves it was a little white lie or have tried to bury the skeletons so far and so deep that no one can find them, there are failures in your past. Yet, God knows your stardom and recognizes you have royalty running in your veins. He chose you. You are God's number one draft pick for the plans and purposes He has for you.

As God chose to love the world, He often teaches us how to love Him through our choices as well. The first and greatest commandment in Exodus 20:3 clearly states, "You shall have no other gods before me." God doesn't make you choose Him, but He gives you free will to respond to His love by accepting it. He fashioned us not to be mere puppets, but He wanted us to understand love as He gives it. God, in His infinite power, understood that you cannot know and understand love if you're forced to give and receive it.

Romans 10:9–10 states, "That if you confess with your mouth, 'Jesus is Lord,' and believe in your heart that God raised Him from the dead, you will be saved. For it is with your heart that you believe and are justified, and it is with your mouth that you confess and are saved." In responding to His love, you acknowledge He is God and that you have sinned, yet by His love your sins are covered infinity times infinity. As you respond in love and obedience to Him, He is able to transform you into what He destined you to be.

He Gave

God established that to love, you must give something of value, something you hold dear, for someone else. Has God ever asked you to give up something you really love? Genesis 22 presents one of the most compelling stories of love. God asked Abraham to sacrifice his son, Isaac, his only son, whom he loved greatly as a demonstration of his love toward God. Whenever God called, Abraham responded immediately and was available for whatever God was calling him to do. Genesis 22:3 says Abraham got up early the next morning and set out. Abraham responded in obedience of love toward God.

Did God really intend for Abraham to kill his son? Absolutely not! God was testing Abraham for idolatry and the condition of his heart so that Abraham, you, and I would know what love toward God looks like. God was testing Abraham to see if Isaac held a greater place in Abraham's heart than God. It's evident that Abraham loved God more. Even after waiting for what seemed like a lifetime for the very thing he so desired, a son, Abraham still found it in his heart to give up the very thing He loved the most. Out of His love toward Abraham, God gave yet again but this time by multiplying Abraham's giving. God not only gave Isaac back, but He also gifted Abraham with a ram in the bush as the redeemer for His love.

Love has to be given away; it's not something you keep all to yourself. When you give, love opens the door to also receive. I'm sure it didn't make a lot of sense to Abraham to give away his only son, but he had grown to be a wise servant and a man of faith. After many encounters of trying to do things his way, Abraham had learned to trust God. We must learn to do the same rather than what seems right to us. As we trust God, we begin to learn His ways, and our ways of thinking begin to dissipate.

He Redeemed

Redemptive love saves; it gives something in place of something else to save another. It will risk its life (i.e., image consciousness, judgment, or even a dying to self) for the cause of the Kingdom. In His infinite wisdom, God knew we wouldn't always get it right. He knew that eventually we'd make a choice that would cause ourselves harm or take us down a path that wasn't His design for us. He was aware of the forces that seek to destroy the purity of His creation. So God fought for us. He was determined that nothing, not anything we could do or any harm intended for us, could separate us from His love. So He sent His son to save us. Christ died to rescue us from ourselves and from a sin-infested world. He freed us from the bondage of death with the enemy and established forever with Him in Heaven.

Have you ever spilled red Kool-Aid on the carpet? If so, you know how hard it was to get that stain out. With the right product and some determined arm action, you could get the carpet looking brand new again. When God's only son, Jesus, died on the cross for our sins, He erased the stains of our sinful life. We are healed by His stripes and have been made whole. He presented us with the opportunity to start a new life, a new beginning.

Dr. Martin Luther King, Jr., one of the most revered, nonviolent civil rights leaders, fought for the many men and women who didn't have the courage or will to fight for themselves. His organized movements were founded on Christian beliefs. From the bus boycott movement that ended the segregation of whites and blacks to the march on Washington, King's years of commitment to equal rights demonstrated one of the greatest expressions of redemptive love. He risked his safety, the security of his family, and the lives of all those who walked with him in the journey so that we would have the freedom to live in a country where African Americans would be respected and regarded as human beings. He fought for equality for everyone.

God is so in love with you that He won't even allow the enemy to have his way with you. He wants you to have your name and story written in Heaven. He's fighting for you. Stop fighting Him. Stop doubting His love. Stop doubting His ability to do Him. His word affirms that He is doing a new thing, nothing that has been done (Isaiah 48:6–7). Isaiah 48:10 says that He's refining you in the furnace of affliction. Let Him love you and do His best work. Verses 17–18 say He knows and will teach you what's best for you and will direct you. Pay attention to His commands lest you desire lack of peace and dissolution.

God is an unconditional God. Stop focusing on your past. It no longer matters. He is out there on the front line fighting for you to make it to the finish triumphantly? He will be your number one cheerleader and usher you to new levels in life. He's shouting, "I love you! You can do it! I believe in you!" He wants so much for you to have the most marvelous life with Him if you just trust Him to do His work in you and make you complete. He will give you chance after chance to get it right. When the cheers don't work and you keep resisting His guidance, He sends you through the fire to push you into your destiny; His love becomes refinement to get you to where He's destined you to be. His love is that magnanimous! Feel worthy of His love; that's why Christ died. It's not a ticket to do whatever you like, but it is an invitation to be your absolute best. Love is you.

WHAT LOVE IS NOT

CHAPTER 1:
LOVE DOES NOT ENVY

*Let us not become conceited, provoking and
envying each other. -Galatians 5:26*

DO YOU FEEL SOME TYPE OF WAY WHEN YOU SEE GOD blessing others? I'm not sure why we compete with one another, why we feel like God or others love someone else more because of what has been given to or done for that person. But what I do know is that love isn't a contest, and envy is a venomous toxin that will rob you of a healthy, fulfilled life. Envy likes to come first and therefore is always focused on a win. It will never be satisfied with anything it perceives as less than. It is self-image driven. Envy wrestles with the fear that it missed out on something or that life hasn't been fair to itself. It fears that there isn't enough of whatever it craves, so it dwells in disbelief and defeat. It operates with a begrudging spirit toward others who are ahead of the curve because those individuals remind it of a seemingly underprivileged place.

When everything around you screams you're not where you'd like to be, it can be a challenge to share in another's happiness. Still, all I can tell you is to find joy in celebrating others anyhow; it will inexplicably help silence the cries of discontent. He says when you are faithful in little, He will promote you to much (Luke 16:10). Don't get tripped up by the fruit you see in someone else's garden, as you have no idea what it took to grow that fruit. If you knew the amount of toil it took to get him or her there, you would find yourself at ease with your current stance.

Envy Feeds the Need for Control

Ironically, for an emotion that is out of control, envy feeds a false need for power. As a result, envy will seek to undermine any good that is being shown toward another. But, what does one really accomplish by looking into someone else's life and blocking favor by trying to control what another person can or cannot have? That's not anyone's decision to make on another's behalf. We don't get to decide another person's fate or happiness. Understand that there is only One in control. Don't get blindsided by ego and judgment. Don't let an ill desire to be on top drive you to hate.

Envy Says I Am the One Who Deserves It

Envy is also about entitlement. Envy asks, "What about my gifts?" Envy says, "I am the one who deserves that blessing." It's an arrogant fixation that the world owes you something. Nobody owes you anything. Love celebrates others and is genuinely happy when something amazing is happening in the life of another, even if that something remarkable hasn't happened for you. And even if that something amazing is happening to someone who has wronged you, love still celebrates. In spite of another person's wrongs, who are we to say they don't deserve God's unconditional love? None of us has the right to say who gets His mercy. Envy can cause you to get all upset about something that has nothing to do with you yet make it about you. Please know it was never meant to be about you. The sooner you can come to that realization, the better you'll be able to find rest for your soul and know real love. What you throw into the universe is often what comes back to you. If you sow resentment toward others, you will find yourself enveloped in a never-ending cycle of bitter comparison. Learn to appreciate what you have. Don't take for granted what's already been given to you.

Envy Operates in Defeat

Envy's address is 0000 Defeat Street. It lives in conquest, yet it doesn't realize that defeat is a mindset. It's always looking in the rearview mirror and focused on where it is in the race. Love is not a race. Love focuses on forward movement, not moving ahead of others. Keep your eyes on the prize.

Envy as a Condition

When you know someone is envious, it's uncomfortable to be in that person's presence because somewhere in it all you know they want to see harm or misfortune shown your way, as envy dislikes anything less than center stage. Because of its hunger for center stage, it's easy to spot when it's not in its "rightful" place. It's hard for envy to share in your gladness. So, genuine support you can forget, since envy and that kind of love mix like oil and water. They just don't coexist well without someone getting hurt. Unconsciously, envy exposes its anxieties but attempts to hide them by thoughts or talks of "He or she thinks they're all that" or "He or she could do it better." It's never about what someone else did to them, but more about what someone else reminds them they are not or what they have not. It's rooted in an unhealthy competition against others, and it won't stop until it has won its game. Living an envious existence can be lonely because no one really has the time or interest to be entertained by something so remedial. Because of its loneliness, it will attempt to provoke you to join in with its shenanigans and invite you to convert to a covetous lifestyle. It's greedy and never focuses on what it does have with gratitude. It's drawn to want and more want. Its thirst is never quenched. Envy says, "I have, but I don't have that, and I would like that."

When I have to visit the doctor for a condition or injury, I always ask the doctor two questions: What is the cause of the issue, and how do I heal and tackle it at the root cause? I ask these questions because I want to understand how I got into the situation to begin with, and I want to do the work to heal and move forward restored. I don't want to mask my condition with Band-Aids or medicines that only treat the symptoms. So it is with envy. It's a condition or injury that must be tackled at the source. Envy is a deep-rooted reflection of who you want to be but for whatever reasons are just not there at the moment. Instead of recognizing that the circumstances are just temporal, you project those feelings of inadequacy or apparent loss onto others when it has nothing to do with the other person. Be careful about wanting what someone has or endeavoring to align your life with theirs. You never know what yoke has been upon them. In everything give thanks, be content, and believe the very best for your life and others.

I have a good friend from college who has been my healthy competition and motivator. We met in the honors program at Langston University our freshman year. Our motivating competition started when we were working on a research paper that we had to submit to the honors program director, Dr. Joy Flasch. He happened to show me his paper before we had to turn it in, and it had these awesome pictures and very organized references to support his paper. I wanted some awesome pictures too, so I went and added pictures to my paper and showed it to him. Well, it was more like, "In your face!" We laughed about it and have always done that for one another, making sure we present the best we have to offer. We have kept that kind of motivation between us over the years, and we often talk about how that kind of friendship has propelled us. Whenever one of us is celebrating a milestone, the other is there front and center. My friend has gone on to do a great many of things in the field of education, and each time we catch up with one another, we share our papers and inquiry about those pictures. If one is looking to be ahead of the other, we ask about those pictures: "Whatcha got now?" I'm thankful that experience has been a motivator for us and not created any malice or envy in our hearts for the other. We want the best for one another and to challenge each other. He's not my only motivator, but he is one of many who has consistently kept me on my toes. Surround yourself with others who don't mind showing you their pictures—how they overcame—and want you to be great. It's easier to be happy for others when they are happy for you when your time comes. And even if they aren't, still celebrate them even if it's just in your prayers. God knows and sees all. Trust that He will reward you in due season. You don't have to worry about your blessings; they will come. You can choose to destroy your spirit by stewing over someone else's blessing, or you can invest that time and energy in loving the One who can change your circumstances and focus on what you can be and do to make your life better. I choose the latter. I would rather have fun making the most of the life He gifted me than wasting time I can never get back resentfully honed in on someone else's divine order.

Choose to focus on your own blessings. Resist the need to compare yourself with others. Instead, focus on being the most amazing you. What is it YOU want to become? Not what is defined by what others are or what they have, but what do YOU want from YOUR life? Take some time to really think and pray about that. If you were given one year to live, what would you do with it? Who would you be? How would you want to leave this world? Then focus on the answer you receive. And if it doesn't come together as you would like it, know that in His eyes it's perfect, and it's still good. I can't tell you why it feels like life seems unfair at times. But one thing I know for sure is that there is a divine plan for it all. You just have to learn how to trust the divine plan. While you're learning, still celebrate you for all that you've become and celebrate others for what God is doing in their lives. I have celebrated others tons in my lifetime.

It's one of my greatest joys. And I'll tell you this: God has always sent the most delightful surprises of support. If those I give to give back, I sincerely appreciate the blessing, as someone's time is a gift and their resources are a double reward. If those I give to don't give back, I no longer worry about it. I used to get my feelings hurt when I didn't know better, but when I made a decision to give God's way, I've never lacked.

The truth is, there are enough blessings to go around for everyone. God, as omnipotent as He is, is able to meet you where you are and bless you beyond your wildest dreams. But you have to do the work to change your circumstance for the better and simply believe. You have to want a future that honestly celebrates others instead of a present that secretly seeks to see others as second best or at their worst.

Love in Action: From Envy to Support

1. Loves does not covet and is not resentful. Ask God to reveal areas in your life where you have been, or are, envious of others and to purge that attitude from your heart and actions.

2. Reflect on your journey and the positive impacts you've made in life. Celebrate those victories with something that brings you personal gratification. It doesn't have to be grandiose; it could be something as simple as writing yourself a thank-you note for all you do for yourself and/or others.

3. Identify someone who has success, whether it's a relationship, a possession, or a dream you admire. Rid yourself of the temptation to compete with him or her. Choose to be genuinely happy for the other person and uplift and support them. Make his or her happiness that of your own.

CHAPTER 2:
LOVE DOES NOT BOAST

For whoever exalts himself will be humbled, and whoever humbles himself will be exalted. -Matthew 23:12

LIGHTS, CAMERA, ACTION! IT IS NOT THE LOUDEST WHO speak with flattering words that show love, but the strength of commitment that doesn't have to say anything, for they show you with their walk, not just their talk.

Love delights in the triumphs of others. It dances at the news of a newborn baby. It rejoices in your singing of a new song yet comforts in songs of sorrow. It enjoys praising the contributions of others. It shows up when you need it most. It puts the interests of others ahead of its own. It's gentle. It's that moment when you realize you were wrong and you have the courage to say, "I apologize." It has no need to shine as to bring attention to itself. Modest love is a quiet confidence. It lends a helping hand to those in need. It doesn't mind being the ghost writer in others' lives. It knows grace and mercy full well and gives it in abundance with an audience of One.

Nonetheless, it is perfectly natural to want to share your joys and blessings with the people around you. We want those whom we love to share in our bliss. God warns, however, of boasting. No one likes a bragger. When your joy of sharing becomes a constant tooting of your own horn, it can cause people to do the exact opposite of what you were aiming to accomplish...boosting your self-esteem. Jeremiah 9:23 states, "Let not the wise man boast of his wisdom or the strong man boast of his strength or the rich man boast of his riches." There is a clear distinction between sharing with others your gladness as a result of God's hand on your life versus bragging about your successes or connections apart from Him. When your sharing honors God, it glorifies His works. Boasting rears its ugly head when you rob God of His glory and take credit for the very thing you're boasting about. It's often disguised as a good deed, but when the mask comes off, you can see that it's merely a cry for appreciation: a cry for elevation based on what you do and who you are presenting yourself to be, but that's not love. Love is not contingent upon how well you can impress others; that's superficiality.

Don't Do It for Show

What is your motivation when you give? Whatever the reasons, don't do it for show. Love doesn't seek attention. 1 Corinthians 13:3 asserts, "If I give all I possess to the poor and surrender my body to the flames but have not love, I gain nothing." Even the most charitable of gestures and sacrificial attempts are meaningless if done for self-promotion. "But when you give to the needy, do not let your left hand know what your right hand is doing, so that your giving may be in secret. Then your Father, who sees what is done in secret, will reward you" (Matthew 6:3–4).

We all want to feel appreciated and celebrated. Though, when you're not feeling appreciated for who you are or recognized for your efforts, bragging can seem like the logical medicinal antidote. As God knows how intoxicating this distorted view of love can be, He warns of such behaviors: "Be careful not to do your 'acts of righteousness' before men, to be seen by them. If you do, you will have no reward from your Father in Heaven. So when you give to the needy, do not announce it with trumpets, as the hypocrites do in the synagogues and on the streets, to be honored by men. I tell you the truth, they have received their reward in full" (Matthew 6:1–2).

God looks at our hearts, not our acts. He says obedience is better than sacrifice. When the need for others to recognize you is greater than the deed itself, your giving is no longer about the act of love; love gives with no conditions for a return on its investment. The investment of love itself is enough reward.

Love Is Not a Contest

When your sharing of achievements is about one-upmanship, that's not love; that's manipulation. There is a difference between encouraging someone to greatness through healthy competition (like that of my college friend and I) and competition that seeks to harm others in a quest to get ahead. Love does not rub its accomplishments in someone else's face to make them feel badly about where they are. Love is not a contest or a debate. It considers others by taking time to invest in their successes. If you know someone is struggling in a certain area, avoid constantly mentioning that area is not a struggle for you. How does that serve you or the other person? That's great that it's not a source of contention for you, but the point is that it is for someone else. Instead of boasting about your position, have a heart that is bent toward the other person. Desire to see them do well and make some steps toward helping them get there. How gratifying would it be to make it to the mountain top together?

A modest heart and spirit cares more about doing the right thing than being right. It's sensitive to the needs of others and lends a listening ear. It's focused on doing good in the world and less about the accolades or need for fame or fortune. It acts out of the goodness of its heart, not for a reward. It understands that only what it does for Christ will last.

Be Careful Not to Boast of Your Gifts or Strengths

Divine gifts don't exempt you from a loveless heart. You can be blessed with amazing spiritual talents; but with a lack of zeal, they become merely superficial traditions or rituals in your life. Performing religious traditions when our hearts are not pure are empty offerings. 1 Corinthians 13:1 points out that you can be gifted in speaking in tongues but without love it's straight noise…annoying and repelling, lacking a sweet melody. It describes such talk as a resounding gong or a clanging cymbal. You can shout about Heaven all day, but your conversation spoken without love is mere emptiness. Further, having the gift of prophecy, understanding and knowledge, even with mustard seed-sized faith, profits no one if arrogance and disdain reign in your heart. "What's love got to do with it?" Absolutely EVERYTHING. We must do our work with a pure heart and do it to honor and glorify God. When our hearts seek to please Him, love will fill our souls and our work then becomes much more powerful and effective here on earth, for we cannot have power without His love.

Moreover, proceed with caution when speaking of your strengths. "So, if you think you are standing firm, be careful that you don't fall" (1 Corinthians 10:12). We can think that it is our weaknesses that cause us to fall prey, but surprisingly it can be our strengths that cause us to stumble. Don't be deceived, as it is in your strengths that you tend to be most relaxed. Your strong suits are also the most attractive to the enemy, as his goal is to weaken your position and prevent you from obtaining the blessings God has for you. If he's not bothering you, either he already has you where he wants you, or it's just a matter of time before he comes knocking at your door. Have the security cameras on standby, and whatever you do, don't answer the knock.

Let Others Praise You

There is nothing like an unsolicited compliment or unexpected praise report from someone other than yourself. However, when that rarely happens, it can be tempting to want to take the mic and make it known what you've done. You then have to ask yourself, did you really do it for the cause? If the answer is a relentless need to share with others about all you've done or how great you are, well then you know where your heart is truly. Solomon encourages the opposite: "Let another praise you, and not your own mouth; someone else, and not your own lips" (Proverbs 27:2).

When you are genuine and your efforts are done with a spirit of reverence toward the Father, people can see that and will innately be drawn to you as a result. They will, without solicitation, want to speak well of you. Even those who might otherwise have spoken negatively will eventually find themselves speaking of the good news of finding and knowing such a rare and humble individual as yourself. Drop the mic and let others praise you. If they don't, speak praises to God.

Boast About His Goodness

"Let him who boasts boast in the Lord" (1 Corinthians 1:31). Brag about His goodness! Tell everyone you meet about His love! Take backstage and shine the spotlight on Him. Make Him the focal point of your success. God loves it when we magnify and bring credit to His name. When we humble ourselves before Him and allow Him to have His rightful place in our lives, there's nothing He won't do for us. His word says that if we delight ourselves in Him, He will give us the desires of our hearts (Psalm 37:4). Honestly, I cannot stop talking about Him (smiling)!

Allow Others to See the Real You

I get it. You want someone to see you, the real you, and still love you. The danger about bragging is that it is an imbalanced portrayal of yourself. Boasting tends to promote only the good, thus tipping the scales of an exaggerated sense of one's self. It creates a misunderstanding that you need an unshared spotlight with an audience of many and can often times come across to others as an annoying need to glorify one's own feats. In its excessive pride, bragging invites others in by attempting to attract only the falsified finer qualities about yourself, but it doesn't allow others to see the total you. Allow others to see the real you. Modest love is not about putting yourself down; it's about being fearless enough to share a balanced view of yourself.

Love in Action: From Boast to Modesty

1. James 4:16 (ESV) describes boasting as arrogant and evil. Pray that God will transcend your heart from the need for others to see only the good in you...that others will see the complete you and still love you. Honor God by giving Him the credit for all that is good in your life.

2. Make a commitment to be true to yourself based on God's truth. Allow yourself to be transparent and share equal scales of yourself with others. Be discerning about who you share the most intimate aspects of yourself with.

3. Choose to boast about the goodness of God and others. Elevate someone who is unassuming, someone who rarely makes any noise, and/or always has a spirit of modesty through speech. Resist the need to include yourself as a contributor to who they are or what they've achieved.

CHAPTER 3:
LOVE IS NOT PROUD

In his pride the wicked does not seek Him; in all his
thoughts, there is no room for God. -Psalm 10:4

Yes to my will, no to your way
I'm the highest of the high, untouchable all day
Superior I stand! Divided I fall? Nah, not me
Always right, you didn't know?
I'm the shine that lights you aglow
My *Merriam-Webster* knows no wrong
Truth is where I'm strong
Game peep game, winning is my title
My silent treatment will turn you idle
My paper is stacked, never ever to know lack
If you make me mad, I may just strike
Go ahead, take a hike
Oh, you don't want me?! NO, you may be dismissed while I get another
My beauty, charm, and intelligence are unmatchable
I stay on the most wanted list
I'd be old and gray, trying to do things God's way
What thus says the Lord? You gotta be kidding me
I'm pride, and I approve this message
                                        -Jacqueline Camphor

PRIDE IS A DANGEROUS FLIGHT TO GET ON. THE danger with pride is that it disconnects you from God because you start believing your survival is all dependent upon you alone. You stop trusting in Him and believing the control is all yours. You buy into the deceptive belief that the source of your successes is a direct result of your solo efforts, but also that everything wrong in your life is your fault. There is a tendency to want to be right always, which often results in the need to have the last word. Everything is a deliberation. Apologies are infrequent and come few in number, as there is rarely anything done on pride's part that requires an admission of guilt. If an apology is rendered, don't get offended if it is not followed up with action, as sometimes the expression of regret was simply to clear pride's conscience. Pride is not likely to see the impact its actions have on others.

Pride designs its own loneliness; it erects isolation in its relationships. It's gotten so used to doing it the "me, myself, and I" way that connection is unfamiliar. It often refers to itself as "just set in my ways," but its real name is unyielding. It can be inflexible at the top (inflated pride) or at the bottom (wounded pride) of its undertaking.

Inflated Pride

Puffed-up, prideful people know it all and feel like they don't need anybody, unless it's someone they deem important to their plans. They are opportunists and love power. They equate superiority as being sovereign. They speak with condescension but present their chitchat as if they are doing something in your favor. In their arrogance, they look down upon others with contempt. Romans 12:3 puts it like this, "Do not think of yourself more highly than you ought, but rather think of yourself with sober judgment, in accordance with the measure of faith God has given you."

God hates pride and clearly expresses its engagement as sin. Pride is the reason Satan fell from God's grace. Don't allow it to get the best of you; allow the best of you to rebuke its worst.

Wounded Pride

Wounded, prideful people want to know connection but lack the ability to attach because they have been hurt deeply. As a result, they are very image conscious and like to appear perfect or elite to the masses. They can come across to others as selfish, but for them it's really about an unconscious self-preservation; for their egotism is founded upon insecurities. The manner in which they interact with others is all about protecting themselves. All in all, wounded pride is still not love, as it blocks any opportunity for intimacy.

To love a prideful person, you must seek to understand than to be understood. They desire to connect on the deepest levels but the moment they see something that reminds them of a past injury, they will find a place back on their throne where they are revered and looked up to. So be ready to invest some considerable time in getting to know them by digging deep. They will tell you what they need if you'll hear what they have to say. Listen attentively to their needs and respond with great tenderness lest you bruise their ego. They need sincere love that supports and believes in their dreams. They can be the most loyal people when they receive loyalty in return.

Vulnerability Is a Virtue

Love requires vulnerability and transparency. It takes just as much strength to be prideful as it does to be vulnerable. The difference is pride takes exhaustive energy while vulnerability takes rewarding energy. Vulnerability allows others to see those things you'd rather keep hidden yet is at peace with the revelation of its imperfections. It opens the door of its heart to permit others to accept it fully and encourages an equal exchange.

Pride has to learn to be vulnerable and allow itself to mature. Even after it's been pushed down, it must learn to get back up and dust itself off and get back in the love of life. Pride has to learn to let go of the control and come down from the throne and just be…whether right, wrong, or indifferent.

Love Allows Itself Help

Your man dives to open the door for you, but you dismiss his efforts with, "I got this." Your woman wants to try to make it work and suggests counseling, but you insist that psychoanalysis is not your thing. Allow yourself help. Love is giving, and giving with a humility of heart is love. When you refuse help, you refuse yourself love. You can't do it all by yourself. And when someone offers to give, accept the gift. Love is not only about giving but also receiving, which is different from taking. Taking sets the tone for what and how it is to receive. Taking seizes its rank by announcing, "This is what I want, and I want you to give it to me. And by the way, that is your job, so no thanks needed." Receiving says, "Yes, thank you. I wasn't expecting anything, yet I won't say no or teach you not to love me in a giving way." It goes on further to say, "I won't block your blessing by preventing the flow of the law of love." The humble allow themselves help.

Humility welcomes wise counsel and support. It knows that there is more than one way to do things and is open to other perspectives. It's smart enough to know God didn't create just one person to have all of life's answers. It doesn't take for granted the love that it is shown but cherishes every kind and thoughtful word, truth, and deed. Whatever it allows to flow in and out of its life is, first and foremost, for the Father. It sincerely considers the benefit of the body of Christ without airs and makes a commitment to play its part with a lasting, careful impact. Therefore, it says no to prideful motives and opens the gates of purity for others who also have a heart for Christ to fulfill the mission and give his or her absolute best for the Kingdom.

Love in Action: From Pride to Humility

1. Ask God to rid your heart of any pride and allow you to be vulnerable with the right people.

2. Choose to let go of the need to be right and resist the desire to have the last word. Take courage in being transparent.

3. Prideful people rarely ask for help or show a side of vulnerability. If you know someone who is prideful, take some time out to find out what's important to him or her and follow it up with an act that shows you were sincerely listening. Show them support without any terms.

CHAPTER 4:
LOVE IS NOT RUDE

To slander no one, to be peaceable and considerate, and
to show true humility toward all men. -Titus 3:2

BAD MANNERS SELL! IN TODAY'S WORLD OF TELEVISION, the bigger the shock and awe, the higher the ratings…the better the business. At some point, we've all been guilty of contributing to this industry sensation by tuning in to a phenomenon for promoting fighting and division as a means of keeping it real. We've savored in the gossip, found humor in the lies, and rallied in the bullying and disrespect. If we care to admit it, it brought some level of enjoyment to watch the embarrassment and dishonor. However, this kind of behavior wounds others and purports to shrink their value. Take a stand and speak up for the alienated. Choose love; choose honor.

On a particular Sunday morning, I had arrived to church earlier than normal. Well, I actually arrived on time. Parking was as smooth as finding me a seat on the end of a row near the front. By the time praise and worship began, our entire section was full. Actually, at that moment, the entire row I was sitting on was full except for the seat to my right. I was blissfully enjoying the worship, and then I found myself distracted by my peripheral vision. There was a man and a woman standing to the left of me in the aisle. The woman was looking at me as if she possibly wanted to ask me something. The man she was with just stood behind her watching. She didn't speak but pointed in my direction as if she wanted to get down the row I was sitting on. I was a bit confused by the request because I saw that there were two of them but only one open seat. I pointed to the seat to my right indicating to her that it was available if she wanted it.

The woman pointed again in my direction. I guess when I didn't catch her gestures, she leaned in to the usher who stood just a couple of feet in front of her. I saw that she was telling him that there were two of them and that they needed two seats. She indicated to him that there was one of me. Because of the music, I couldn't hear their entire conversation but got the gist of what she was now asking or suggesting of him to do, so I pointed again to the seat next to me and raised one finger to her and the usher to indicate that there was only one free seat. I could see him listening attentively to her petition. What I did finally hear loud and clear was the usher's response: "Ma'am, I'm sorry." He was trying his best to be kind to her while communicating to her that he couldn't help her make me move my seat, especially when there were no other seats in the section.

The two were late, and she completely interrupted worship service to promote her own agenda. I was thankful the usher so gently stopped her in her mission because this woman was determined and wasn't leaving until she had those two seats. It was clear she was oblivious to the gravity of what she was requesting. She never once stopped to consider me, or anyone else for that matter.

Consider Your Circle of Influence

No matter the plethora of kind words people say to you behind closed doors, you will know how they truly feel when they are in the presence of others. When given the opportunity to esteem you in front of others, do they speak well of you, or do they rally behind the naysayers and jump on the roasting bandwagon? Beware of those who seek to elevate themselves at the expense of ruining your reputation or holding you back from greatness. Those who are clearly on your team will reverence your name whether or not you're present. They will speak in the affirmative on your behalf, not because you are without faults, but because they choose to focus on your goodness. Accordingly, consider a sphere of influence that respects others and wants to see others finish well. Likewise, be a positive ambassador for them also.

Pour Cold Water on Gossip

Gossip can be an alluring and tempting pastime in which to participate. It starts out like a warm, simmering campfire but gets hotter with every harmful word that is spread. Before it burns you, pour cold water on it! Proverbs 11:13 states, "A gossip betrays a confidence, but a trustworthy man keeps a secret." I know how juicy of a melody gossip can be to the ear, but it can sour the soul and entangle you in a web of woes if you surrender to its call. Just say, "No!" Unless it is a life-threatening matter, if someone confides in you with something near and dear to him or her, cherish that trust and take care in protecting their privacy to the grave. Even in a life-threatening situation, be sensitive about involving the right people and ensuring they have a sincerity to help versus just needing to be nosey. My father would say, "If you don't want anyone to know anything, don't share it. If it was too juicy for you to hold, how do you expect someone else to hold it?" How would you feel if your most treasured trust was broken as a result of a confidence shared or lies spread that could harm your future? Once it's out there, it's out there. To right the wrong would be like trying to remove daggers from a bleeding heart.

If They Can't Beat You, They'll Join You

Crudity loves companionship, though it's tough to keep impolite company when there is no one to share an ill-mannered performance. Therefore, the best way to defuse a bomb of boorishness is not to alight. Sometimes it can be difficult not to react to the blatant disrespect of others. But you relinquish your crown for power when you respectively decline to be a codependent in others' issues. It takes a great deal of fortitude and maturity to walk away from intended harm and be a part of the resolve. What you respond to is what you attract. It may appear that they've won, but the true determinant of a winner is character. By ignoring their negative invitation for attention, they are forced to look for a different kind of attention. When they find that you don't respond to foolish antics, they will have no choice but to leave you alone or fall in line. Either way, they will end up joining you in the agreement that it's not worth your time, nor your life.

Consider Their Pain

When a person's pain is great, it has the tendency to affect others in the most uncouth ways. Consequently, all rude behavior is not a plot to kill your spirits; it's not a conspiracy. Sometimes people are quietly living in a painful place and are looking for a way to heal their own hurt. From their careless whispers to their shameless plugs to build themselves up, they are attempting to rid themselves of all the dirt and debris they've kept swept under the rug of their front porch…the stuff they've tried to keep other folks from seeing. You just happened to be the person walking by when it happened. Don't let their spring cleaning make you believe that it is a personal vendetta against you. It's not personal.

I hold the covenant of marriage in high esteem and promote togetherness and commitment when it comes to the marital union. I used to get perturbed when certain women would treat me as if I was interested in their husbands even when I knew nothing about their husbands. The looks were saddening at times. When I realized the looks had nothing to do with me per se but more about what was going on behind closed doors…the dirt and debris, I gained a sense of compassion for those women. I think if we learned to put ourselves in the shoes of someone else, we would have a greater knowledge for who people are and would have less misunderstandings. Don't stop caring. Grab a dustpan instead of getting aroused unnecessarily.

Your Honor Has Power

You can influence healing when you respond to disrespect with nobility. Rather than returning an offense with an unkind offense, try honor. You honor others by how you treat them, so be mindful of your conduct. On many occasions, I've seen a person who intended to harm others would be the same person who would need help from those they weren't kind to. Most people, on the other hand, don't intend to be rude or mean, but in the midst of the flight and fast pace of life, sometimes that's just what it is but has nothing to do with you. You were once in that place of rushing and being unaware, so serve up some honey as opposed to hate.

You honor a person by being specific about their contributions to this life. Surround yourself with those who honor and respect you, who speak life into you, and who share in your successes. For who you surround yourself with is who you eventually become. Critical spirits only stifle your creativity and free-spiritedness, so find those who will make the investment in you to help take you to new levels and champion your flight.

Words have great power, so love enough to think before speaking. "Show proper respect to everyone: love the brotherhood of believers, fear God, honor the king" (1 Peter 2:17). Choose words that bless and inspire, as once they've hit the airways, you can't take them back. Choose to speak well of everyone and ill of no one. Focus on the attributes and qualities in people that mirror God's light. When you focus on the good in others, the qualities that may not appear as love-able begin to diminish. As you shine a light on them, their love begins to shine back on you. Your love for them is not about what isn't, but rather about what is. Your love becomes healing and strength and circumvents courage in others to love in return.

Love in Action: From Rude to Honor

1. Pray that God will surround you with people who honor and esteem you and others. Pray that you will be that for others as well.

2. Choose not to participate in gossip going forward no matter how juicy.

3. As you encounter rude behavior, make a decision not to partake in the disrespect. Choose honor over returning an offense. Speak well of others in spite of any mistakes they've made.

CHAPTER 5:
LOVE IS NOT SELF-SEEKING

Do nothing out of selfish ambition or vain conceit, but in humility consider others better than yourselves. -Philippians 2:3

EVERYTHING THAT THE FATHER DID OUT OF LOVE WAS for the good of others. If you want someone to see you, you have to see others. "Do not neglect to show hospitality to strangers, for thereby some have entertained angels unawares" (Hebrews 13:2 ESV). Sometimes we can get so caught up in our own press that we forget others have press too.

Love is knowing your worth and what you have to give to the world, not what you think the world owes you or what you're entitled to. Everyone has some level of selfish tendencies, but a self-seeking love knows no boundaries. When love is all about me, myself, and I, your view of love is one-sided. Learn that it's not about you.

Selfish Love

Want to know if you have an "it's all about me" attitude? Listen to your conversations. Look to see who is carrying the weight of the relationship in terms of trying to keep it together. The person who is always demanding and taking is typically the one who is making it about self. When it's all about the other person, you will put less on them. Love your relationship enough to give it more.

We make the biggest mistakes in relationships when we don't love people for who they are. Selfish love will attempt to fit another person into a mold. It says, "You're not enough as you are; therefore, here is the blueprint for you to be good enough for me." It will try to change you to be what it wants. Is there someone in your life you're trying to change? Is someone trying to change you? A lot of the struggles we have in relationships are because we're trying to change one another, and it's not only selfish but counterproductive to the relationship. Chances are those attempts to change are more about the person trying to usher transformation. For a self-seeker, if he or she gets what they want from their love relationship, the blessing is great. However, if the person they claim to love never becomes what they want, the fabricated need to change the other person will overshadow all happiness. Yes, you should indeed help those in your life to be better, but do so with an open invitation and not to their embarrassment. Help them be better, but you have to be your best self before they can know and see what "better" looks like. If you take an honest look at yourself, there are some things you need to work on. Take the changing to God and watch Him work.

When you're constantly looking to the other person to change or show you love, it is likely that your priority of love is out of order. It could be that, selfishly, you're looking to your loved one to be your little god; don't expect your loved one to be your god. No one person will ever be able to fulfill all your hopes and dreams, so don't do that to anyone. That's a very heavy role for anyone. When your loved one doesn't act or treat you the way you believe he or she should, talk to God about it before you do anything else. A lot of times we're looking for the other person to be God in our lives when there's only one God, so we must look to Him for love. Outside of that, it may be your own selfishness on the rise.

It's natural to be drawn to someone who has given you a kind smile or an encouraging word. The error of self-seeking love is that its desire for more of what it was instinctively drawn to dominates the love relationship. Selfish love will give to get. In the beginning, it can appear to be the most amazing kind of love until self-seeking love doesn't get its way. When it doesn't, you will need to take cover, or you will get swept up in its destructive winds. It will drain you of your dignity and render you great turmoil as it places judgment on the love you give to it in return. It places stipulations on what is good love. If what you're giving doesn't line up with good loving, it will try to shame you into giving back until it feels good about itself and your relationship again. Love is not manipulative and does not place ill conditions on how the other person is supposed to love you. What seemingly started out as love on a two-way street turned into an avenue of one-way demands to feed an ego. Self-seeking love will drain the one it claims to love. Although it does show some level of love and affection, its expression of love is always done with half efforts; yet, its expectation of the other person is to always go in all the way. That's not love. That's a greedy motivation to be esteemed. I encourage you not to be controlled by its trickery, for what you feed your soul is what wins. Be careful about your consistent association with self-seeking love, as it can poison your spirit. It can rob you of your joy and slowly cook you into that thing you grow to distaste.

Selfless Love

The most successful relationships I've experienced have been the ones that give, the ones that selflessly consider others and love with no strings attached. Selfless love values your time. It considers the commitments of others and seeks to understand and compromise rather than assert its own agenda. It is fully aware of what hurts you and does its best not to send disappointment your way. It prays for you and wants the very best for you, even if that best doesn't include itself. Selfless love uplifts and makes its intentions known and follows through with promising action.

To love someone truly, learn to listen and sincerely consider the other person. You have to listen as much as you share and respect and support the other person. Consider that just because it's good or best for you doesn't make it best or good for someone else. It takes selfless love to let go of the position of priority number one and allow someone else to have that position in its place. And more often than not, it takes selfless love to give someone else a love greater than they've ever known.

A deep, loving friendship and relationship takes time to develop; it's not rooted in the highs of emotional feelings, likes, and passions. If it's all emotional (roller coaster), it's usually about self and not the other person. When there's a peace, it's because we've learned to give to the other without expecting anything in return.

Don't get so wrapped up in your plans for a relationship that you neglect to ask God for His plans. You may have thought you were having the time of your life until you let go of your plans and allowed Him to implement His. Learn to let go of the outcome and rest in Him. Learn how to really love a person beyond the emotional stuff. Know how to love others better while still choosing to love Him more. Learn how to uplift others and to live in peace. Choose to give love without anticipating anything back or peeking around the corner for more.

Love in Action: From Self-Seeking to Consideration

1. Ask God to reveal any blind spots where you have made things more about you and less about others. Make the necessary changes to have a heart of compassion for others.

2. Do something for someone else, and do it with joy. Go out of your way to stand in the gap for someone else or help lighten someone's load. Don't expect a thank-you.

3. Consider a charitable need that is near and dear to your heart. Give at least an hour of your time (not only money) in service to that organization.

CHAPTER 6:
LOVE IS NOT EASILY ANGERED

*Do not be quickly provoked in your spirit, for anger
residues in the lap of fools. -Ecclesiastes 7:9*

DISAPPOINTMENT IS WHEN EXPECTATION MEETS A lesser reality. Anger takes the disappointment of an expectation to unyielding high degrees. It is an irrational, emotional reaction to what it believes to be a major offense. Anger is a short-circuited inability to effectively communicate a need. It's a stubborn frustration that centers on the negative and refuses to let go of its certainty that someone or something is out to get it. Anger gets off on what it perceives to be an infringement upon its time, bad manners, rudeness, impatience, stupid questions, or criticism. Anger always assumes what was done was done with an intent to hurt and that it's being attacked. In its immaturity, anger has a childish requisite to not only win the fight but to be celebrated for doing so. A crisis crier, it lacks the ability to respond with a solution. A solution is almost never foreseeable because often times anger looks only at a small facet of the circumstance when there is a much bigger cause in view. Anger's ability to accelerate from zero to one hundred is faster than a Porsche 918 Spyder and will continue to increase in fury at the tiniest of transgressions.

Do you know someone who, without fail, gets upset at the smallest of things? Even when all that surrounds them is good, they just can't seem to get past reacting to everything in the negative? Worse yet, have you ever been in a relationship where you were constantly having to watch your words or actions for fear of being misunderstood? Even in your best efforts, nothing you did or said was ever good enough, and the person seemed to constantly get upset with you? It's not a good feeling being in an unending cycle of commotion. Moreover, it's depleting to feel like you're being manipulated or controlled by someone's rage.

This happened to Brenda. Brenda and Cindy had been friends for several years. However, no matter what Brenda did for Cindy, it was never enough. After learning that Cindy had taken on the role as a caregiver, Brenda thought she would be a supportive friend by helping to lighten her load. Just when Brenda thought she had done something nice for Cindy, Cindy would make it known she didn't approve. This constant cycle of "thanks, but no thanks" continued for some time until Brenda had had enough. What started out as Brenda giving of her time to help a friend later became a progression of requests for help that went unappreciated. To prevent herself from experiencing further mistreatment, Brenda chose to remain calm yet began telling Cindy "no" to the requests for help. Proverbs 17:27 states, "A man of knowledge uses words with restraint, and a man of understanding is even-tempered." Rather than retaliate in anger, Brenda chose to pray for Cindy about how she was responding to her support. Although Brenda still helps out on occasion, it's not nearly as much as she had in the past. Interesting enough, Brenda now sees a positive change in Cindy. Cindy has since expressed a greater sense of gratitude for what Brenda does for her. Brenda says, "She's watching God change the heart of her friend, while also allowing Him to change her own heart."

Eric and Tonya, who had been married for many years, experienced a similar situation. Eric was raised in a household where criticism and judgment were the norm, but they were not something he wanted for his own family. When he married Tonya, she projected more of what he didn't like about his upbringing. From his vantage point, she was always nagging him, and he saw it as annoying and disrespectful—"A quarrelsome wife is like a constant dripping" (Proverbs 19:13). Instead of sharing his heart with Tonya about the things she did that hurt him, he would bottle his anger and built up resentment toward her. When injury is staring insult in the face, you must make it a priority to deal with the offense by not making a bad situation worse, or it will grow like a cancer and poison the very essence of your being. "In your anger do not sin; do not let the sun go down while you are still angry" (Ephesians 4:26).

Unfortunately for Eric and Tonya, his anger and resentment grew until all he had for Tonya was repaid hurt. "A fool gives full vent to his anger, but a wise man keeps himself under control" (Proverbs 29:11). Some years later, their marriage would end in divorce. Like many former marriages, theirs could have possibly been saved if Eric and Tonya had both learned to communicate in an effective and loving way. They gave in to their wrath until the pain was so great that, in their mind, they had reached a point of no return.

We must forgive. Without forgiveness, you will live a life of regret. Harboring anger and resentment is repelling to those around you, but even love doesn't allow us to give up on seeing the worst in one's self become something greater. Don't miss out because of your prejudgments of what love is. Philippians 4:8 says, "Finally, brothers, whatever is true, whatever is noble, whatever is right, whatever is pure, whatever is lovely, whatever is admirable—if anything is excellent or praiseworthy—think about such things." Forgiveness is one of the best displays of love you can give, not only to others but also to yourself, because without peace it will always be a turbulent flight. A person's attempt to right a wrong should be followed by an immediate admission of error and action of correction and repentance. Forgiveness is a setup for a great testimony to honor and glorify God.

Sometimes we hold back love, thinking we're punishing the other person when we're really only punishing ourselves. It's not your job to chastise anyone, let alone another adult. That kind of bad behavior is driven by the need to control the response of others rather than your own dysfunctional reaction. Not only that, but you will find your spirit in a knot trying to make people something they simply are not. You can't expect others to make you happy, but things can turn around if God ordains it. Keep loving, trusting, and believing. Don't allow your mistakes and the mistakes of others to take you down a path of destruction. "If your brother sins against you, go and show him his fault, just between the two of you. If he listens to you, you have won your brother over" (Matthew 18:15). Most of all, seek peace first.

The next time you're tempted to react to an offense, have some self-control; show grace. "A gentle answer turns away wrath, but a harsh word stirs up anger" (Proverbs 15:1). Stop for a moment to consider what the other person may be experiencing. Don't just stop at the first chapter; read the whole book. Their bad day (the one impacting you) could be the result of something deeply buried. So keep calm, and be kind. Remember that the ultimate goal is connection. Choose happiness; anger doesn't live here anymore.

Love in Action: From Anger to Self-Control

1. Submit to God any feelings of anger and resentment you have toward another. Ask Him to help you to be slow to speak and quick to listen. Ask Him to teach you how to respond in peace and not react in turmoil.

2. Spend ten minutes in self-meditation daily. Find a quiet place where you will not be interrupted. Rid your thoughts of all the noise and distractions and focus your mind on good thoughts. Visualize an optimistic future and find hope in that.

3. Make a commitment to think before reacting to an offense. Consider how your response can help you win as a team, then respond in love.

CHAPTER 7:
LOVE KEEPS NO RECORD
OF WRONGS

*If any one of you is without sin, let him be
the first to throw a stone.* -John 8:7

IN THE WORLD IN WHICH WE LIVE, THERE WILL BE
people who are waiting for you to make a mistake so they may enjoy
reading the headlines. Keeping score is for sports, not for relationships. Love does not play games. People make mistakes. She may
forget to pick up the clothes from the cleaners for that all-important
business engagement. He may have forgotten to take out the trash.
The kids will eventually break something that has sentimental value.
A friend may even take you for granted. Nevertheless, how you see
the mistake is what determines the course of your relationships. Do
you view them as earth shattering or as a minor disappointment?
Are you keeping score for every time a mistake is made? If you want
to position your relationships for demise, keep making mounds into
mountains. Even in athletics, they teach sportsmanlike conduct and
how to play fair. So, who cares if he forgot to take out the trash or
that she forgot to make a run to the cleaners. There are worse things

in life, like people dying from war. Don't turn what was initially miniscule into something so massive.

Love doesn't play the blame game. It doesn't blame others for an alleged wrong or everyone else for what isn't good in its life. More than that, love certainly doesn't blame God, the Author and Creator of love. When you look at others and are constantly finding fault, maybe what you see is really what you dislike about yourself being mirrored to you in others. It's easy to focus on the shortcomings of other people, but it keeps you in a state of self-righteousness.

Love is allowing others to make mistakes and giving them the grace and mercy to fall and get back up. It still expects the best yet doesn't kick them down further because we all have fallen. Love doesn't give up; it gives the one who needs understanding an opportunity and a chance (i.e., lesson, growth, or maturity) to get it right. Love doesn't seek to retaliate because it received something that didn't look like love; it just loves. Love doesn't react or seek to get even; it just loves. Love also trusts and believes and is patient. Love prays for you and wants the very best for you because without love, what is life, really? Love doesn't hold you too tightly; it lets go so you can grow and find your own way back to love.

Do you realize how much energy it takes to hawk on the negative and the misfortune of others? It's majorly tiring and profoundly unhealthy. It's like trying to address and uproot every weed that takes sprout in someone else's life rather than nurturing with good soil, fertilizer, and refreshing waters. When people don't meet your expectations, try not to complain or trample them with insults. Criticize the efforts, and you will kill the spirit of the giver. Be sensitive about making people feel like what they do for you is their job. When you do this, you are saying to them that you take them for granted. Respect the person in front of you enough to at least say thank you. If they are making an effort to love, celebrate the victories whether great or small. Learn to consider the endeavor of the other. It truly is the thought that matters most because no one has to think about you. The more you appreciate others, the more likely they are to want to do for you. The more you treat them like it's their responsibility or duty to love you, especially when you show them little appreciation, the less likely they will have a zeal or desire to do anymore.

If you're expecting your relationships to be perfect, you clearly don't know and understand relationships. Perfectionism is a waste of love. God's love does not depend on what you do or don't do. If you think God loves you only in your perfection, then you'll only see love in that regard and always feel like you can make no mistakes. You will also love yourself that way and express the same toward others. Love adores flaws and imperfections. That is why Christ died, and that demonstration of love perfects us all.

You never know what cross people bear. Don't add to the weight by inflicting more pain and heartache. When your aim is always about trying to teach someone a lesson, it may be to you whom the lesson is taught. That effort to try to return hurt may end up backfiring.

We want to focus on what the other person did to us, but what about what you did to yourself. Take responsibility for what you enabled. Now, that doesn't mean you go into each relationship with a wall up, but guard your heart. Don't beat yourself up because God's grace is sufficient.

There were times in my relationships where something was done for me that I didn't ask for, yet I was reminded of the "gift" or when I fell short of their expectations. Those relationships taught me not to make mistakes. They also taught me not to ask for help, for if that is how I would be treated by not asking for help, I could only imagine what it would be like if I did. We have to be careful about hanging commitments over others' heads or making people feel indebted. Does he or she remind you of everything they've done for you? Are you punishing or being punished for the mistakes of someone else? Don't let other people reprimand you for choices they made in their lives.

I have always been the kind of person that kept my commitments. If I told someone I was going to be there for them, I was, no matter how difficult it was to squeeze into my schedule. I've had to cancel a few commitments recently because I just overextended myself or even double-booked myself. I felt bad for having to cancel, as that had never been my MO, but the love that was shared despite having to scratch the plan has changed me. When people understood, it made me want to love them more. And when they still supported me despite it all, I knew it was just God walking me through the vision—His design for love.

Instead of focusing on the wrongs of others, share more "I love yous!" Appreciate those who realized they made a mistake and apologized before you could ever utter a word about it. Then turn around and do the same for someone else. Be thankful for the friends and family who have stuck by your side and didn't abandon you for something you may have said or done, especially the unawares. Then turn around and gift someone else with an unconditional commitment to stand by their side. Love knows no boundaries.

Love in Action: From Wrongs to Compassion

1. Ask for forgiveness for all the wrongs you have ever committed (Psalm 51 is a great prayer on forgiveness). Forgive yourself for your part in the wrong. Then, let it go and don't look back.

2. Allow yourself the freedom to make mistakes, just try not to keep making the same mistakes. A mistake means you tried and didn't hit the bull's-eye; next time get closer to the bull's-eye until you do. Whatever you do, don't stop trying!

3. Gift someone with the peace of making a mistake or just being imperfect. Offer your help. Allow the imperfection to draw you closer versus further away.

CHAPTER 8:
LOVE DOES NOT DELIGHT IN EVIL

Do not be overcome by evil, but overcome
evil with good. -Romans 12:21

PEOPLE AREN'T BAD; THEIR CHOICES ARE. THE SUM OF our choices is how we've lived. Evil is "live" spelled backward; it's love turned upside down. Where evil exists, love cannot. People who delight in evil choose not to live. They choose to operate in battle with a mission to destroy all that has or hasn't hurt them because that is what they believe love for themselves is. They have been severely harmed at some point, or repeatedly, and the space they operate in is normal to them.

Part of the harm they have experienced is their own decision to exist in a dark place. Evil is a mindset. As I'm continuing to grow in my love, I'm seeing that a lot of what we call evil is badly damaged hearts. We've all heard the saying, "Hurt people hurt people." They are just doing what they believe is protecting themselves.

The thing about evil is that it can trip you up and have you believing that you deserve it. It will make you think it's your fault that you are in the situation you are. It will play on your kindness and loyalty. Its mission is to control; it will seek to alienate you and cause you to eliminate any healthy relationships in your life. Its goal is to break you of anything that is good.

You can win the battle over evil by returning to it goodness. Nonetheless, don't mistake responding with goodness as being a pushover. You can respond in love by giving kindness in a way that still respects self.

Deception

Deception can present itself in a myriad of forms in your relationships. More often than not, however, you will be able to identify the trickery if you pay attention and simply listen. There will be signs, some as clear as "Beware of Danger," while others may say "Proceed with Caution." No matter the signs, they will be there, but where you end up is dependent upon whether you stop or slow down to read them. What you choose will then be in your court, and in the end, you can't say you didn't know because the signs were there. If you're truly honest with yourself, you knew, but you didn't really want to know because you wanted what you wanted. No one, not even the signs, were going to stop you from getting to where you were trying to go. When you take the wheel over from the Owner (God) and are so focused on your destination, you can miss some much-needed guidance. As a result, you may end up somewhere you never wanted to be, somewhere dark and desolate, yet all the while blaming others for not telling you about the signs. You deceived yourself, not anyone else.

Other times, deception is just really good. So, if you're all heart and no thought, you will be turned on your head wondering, "What did I miss? Where did I go wrong?" Deception talks a great game and loves to shower you with lip service, but it never really has any true action behind its words. It loves to reel you in and get your heart fluttering. Once it knows it has your heart, you've moved from potential to prey.

We have been told a million times that love is a game and that we must play the game to get what we want. Um, so how is that working out for you? Don't be deceived; duplicity is a thief, and lying will kill trust. Deception will attempt to play the game so well that it robs you of your choice. Love does not take away one's freedom to choose. Deception will then have the nerve to show you its hand after it's played you. Be mindful that duplicity may have caught him or her, but it won't keep them. Whatever you do, don't lie; tell the truth, as the real you must and will show up. If you arrived into a relationship by deceit, ask the Father to heal and surrender your heart to Him. I pray your loved one has enough heart to accept you fully.

Character, almost always, is a sure tell all for whether he or she is who they say they are. If he makes a promise, how easy is it to break that promise? If she says she's an honest person, how does she handle the situation at the cash register when the clerk gives her more cash than she is owed? Are they always looking for a hook-up, or are they willing to pay their own way. These may seem like little things, but the little things say big things about one's integrity. If something is tugging at you about a person, take time to find out what that tug is about. Inquire about the character of a person as well as his or her story. It will tell you a lot. Don't inquire to get gossip; inquire to make an informed decision about whether to love them up close or from a distance.

Addiction

Addiction is not love. It's an unhealthy desire for something or someone it believes can rescue it of its pain. It's a desperate, numbing need for gratification and control. Its highs are only temporary and keep it coming back for more. It will try to put its victims in a box for fear that they will not love it and/or love outside its borders. Without the control, it believes no one will see it. It doesn't realize that pain won't kill but addiction can. Sober judgment will be its only remedy.

Addiction is desperate. Desperation says, "I don't believe I'm worthy, so please make me worthy." It's pleading for you to love it all because it's bought into the lie that if you love it, it will magically be made whole. But when we love out of order, even all of the love from someone else won't necessarily heal us. Sometimes helping is not helping. Loving is not enabling, but rather it requires you to participate and take responsibility for your actions. Love is action.

Addiction can find a sparkling diamond in the rough quite appealing because everything it has known has been the opposite of good. It doesn't believe it can have the diamond or likely even deserves it. So it will, by any means necessary, take whatever it can get. What does it have to lose when anything is better than its known existence? If it takes hold of the diamond, it will likely break it because it is inexperienced in something that wonderful.

Addiction doesn't respect "no" as an answer. It sees it as a challenge. Love respects your "no" (i.e., your "no" to graciously decline an invitation for a romantic relationship, "no" to sex outside of God's design, or "no" to a financial hook-up). If someone doesn't respect your "no," you will battle with them over the need to control you. Even God doesn't control you. He gives you the free will to choose Him...to love Him back.

Abuse

I don't believe in giving up on people. However, there is a fine line between giving up on people and cutting your losses. There are just some people you have to love at a distance for your own personal well-being and/or safety. If she speaks to you with words that are aimed to intentionally kill your spirits, that is her issue, not yours. If he hits you, that is his fault, not yours. If he hits, you must take care of you; take refuge and make the necessary changes in your life to make sure you are getting the best kind of love. As loving as God is, I don't believe He wants us to suffer at the hands of someone else. He calls us to a life of worth; that's why He died, so we could know His abundant love. I believe we would dishonor His legacy by accepting anything less than His best for our lives.

Lira is one of many who has had to grapple with the evils and repercussions of abuse. As a result, she had to make a tough, but loving decision to remove herself from a marriage of mistreatment. It involved years of healing, reconciliation, and forgiveness.

Lira's Story

Forgiveness is different for everyone, depending on their situation. For me, it was a process that took ten years. I met my ex-husband through his cousin who attended my same high school. When I met him, I was an impressionable fourteen-year-old who had been reared in a strict upbringing and Indian culture. He was seven years older than I was, and I thought I was "in love."

I was married to my high school sweetheart right after I graduated. The first few years of our marriage were great, and he was everything I wanted in a partner. When I met him, I knew he used recreational drugs, but I had never witnessed it. He had promised me that he had quit. But I caught him red-handed one day using drugs with his buddies. We were going to one of his friend's house, but he demanded that I stay in the car because it wasn't going to take him very long. I waited for fifteen minutes, and I got out of the car and went inside and saw him using the drugs. He saw me and asked, "What are you doing here when I asked you to stay in the car?" At that moment, I realized that he was never going to change with regard to using recreational drugs. When we were leaving his friend's house, he said that if I told anyone, which included his family, I would regret it. But, as we were approaching our five-year anniversary, we were starting to drift apart; we were barely communicating, and he started obsessing over whom I was with at work and school. His obsession with wanting to know whom I was hanging out with got worse, and he became very paranoid. With him becoming more and more obsessive, I was afraid that he might actually carry out his threats to hurt me. The pressure to have kids from his family didn't help the situation. I was still trying to go to school part-time while working full-time.

What made me realize that he wasn't going to change, period, was when he threatened my life. We were walking out of my office, and there were some police offers standing nearby. He said, "If you tell those police officers anything (about the threats made), I will kill you because I have a gun in the car." I was scared, and the police officers saw the fear in my eyes. The officers asked if there was anything wrong or bothering me, so I told them yes and that my husband had just threatened my life with a gun. So the police officers escorted us to the parking lot to make sure there was not a gun in the car. After searching the car, the police officers asked if I had a place to go, anywhere besides home, and I said yes. They didn't find a gun, but I decided to separate from him.

After this latest situation, I moved into an apartment and was contemplating whether to start the divorce proceedings or to give him another chance. I was very stressed and had started experiencing severe headaches as a result. I was at my doctor's appointment for a checkup when he asked if there was anything bothering me. I told him yes and that I needed to make a life-changing decision. By the time I left my doctor's office, I had made the decision to start the divorce proceedings. I contacted my attorney, but he could not serve the divorce papers. My husband gave one address or another to avoid being served. This charade went on for a few weeks, and whenever he called me, I would literally beg him not to avoid being served with the papers and asked him nicely to sign the papers so that we could continue to move forward. Finally, a hearing was set and we appeared in front of the judge to grant me the divorce, since it was uncontested. The judge ordered us to try to work things out by giving us eight weeks to see if things changed. When December 1995 rolled around and my court date to finalize was nearing, I was anxious because I just knew he would have something up his sleeve that might cause the judge to deny the divorce. To my surprise, he abided the judge's request, and we appeared again in front of the judge. The judge asked us if we had tried everything to work things out before he would consider granting me the divorce. I told the judge we had, and the divorce was granted in December 1995.

During my marriage, I was verbally, physically, and emotionally abused. Before even starting the divorce proceedings, I had suggested we try marriage counseling. At first, he was not going to talk to a shrink about our marriage. He kept saying "real" men didn't do that. I told him that if he wanted to try saving our marriage he needed to put aside his macho-ness and be open-minded to the suggestion. He finally agreed to marriage counseling. He went once and said that it wasn't for him. I continued going for my own benefit. I continued the therapy sessions to help me heal and move forward.

I thought I would never contact my ex-husband again because the last few years of our marriage were not pleasant, and he had immediately remarried. For some reason as I was approaching my ten-year anniversary of being divorced, I kept thinking that I wanted closure and forgiveness. This feeling kept nagging at me, so I contacted him to meet somewhere to chat. On the day we were supposed to meet, he said he couldn't because his current wife didn't think it was a good idea, and he wanted to respect their marriage vows and avoid any stress. I said that was fine and didn't want to cause any trouble for him. After I got off the phone, I told myself that I forgave him and had my closure and could move forward. After getting the closure, I continued to see the therapist to help me accept the closure. I continued the sessions to gain an understanding of things I could have possibly done differently as well as things I could do better in the future. I learned that I didn't always have to try to please everyone and that the best love I could give myself was mutual respect and understanding through loving communication and trust.

In conclusion, I realized that forgiveness and closure come in many forms, and there's no deadline to achieve that because it's different for everyone. Moving onward, I felt a sense of peace from within. My friends would ask, "Why would you forgive someone who brought you terrible pain?" I would tell them, "So that I could continue to move forward. I can forgive, but I won't forget." The whole experience was therapeutic for me, and I now take the good and bad things from a relationship as a learning experience and continue to grow in my life.

Revenge

Revenge is a danger zone. "Do not take revenge, my friends, but leave room for God's wrath, for it is written: 'It is mine to avenge; I will repay,' says the Lord" (Romans 12:19). God was warning against the dark desire to seek revenge on others who have wronged us. He knew what it would do to our hearts and the high cost we would have to pay if we entered into such a blood-stained battle. Vengeance says more about the person seeking payback than the person who established the fault. Revenge creates this never-ending cycle of an eye for an eye, and the ripple effect of consequences is crushing. It's deceptive; it makes you think you'll be satisfied after you're able to get even, but it's wrong. You will end up down a path of no return unless you seek God. At the end of the day, someone must raise the white flag to end the blood bath. We have no right to judge anyone let alone decide any type of consequence on their life. Unless your life role is rooted in the justice system, we must give the offense over to God. Even in the justice system, decisions to settle the score should be done with prayerful guidance.

The best revenge is to be your best self while others are trying to bring you down. Even greater revenge is to love your perpetrator until they're overwhelmed with kindness. It's so much fun to confuse the enemy like that. Love will kill a multitude of offenses. Sometimes, you will just encounter those who haven't learned what it means to love. That doesn't mean you have to be mean or rude as a result. Their ability to know of a God who loves them may be a result of who you represent in Christ, so represent firmly yet gently.

Don't give energy to the negativity. There will be many things that will try to steal your love. Recognize that it's all a distraction to keep you divided. When you're at odds with those you love, take a moment to consider the issue. What is the problem? What are you really fighting about? What you are facing could be nothing more than the enemy pitting you against one another. It could be nothing more than the enemy attempting to rob you of your harmony. And if you give in to the constant need to win or need to have the last word, you will sabotage your peace. You will enjoy seeing your loved one hurt because they intentionally or unintentionally hurt you. The more and more you fight, the more comfortable you will get with this cycle. The more it becomes a common place for you. Every day you choose who you want to be by what you do.

Love in Action: From Evil to Good

1. Ask God to restore any brokenness in your life as a result of evil attacks. Pray for those who have meant or caused you harm. Ask for forgiveness for any harm you have caused others.

2. Choose to take heed of the warning signs. Love yourself enough not to allow deceptive, addictive, abusive, or vindictive spirits to poison your soul.

3. When tempted to get even with someone for something they did to harm you, just don't. Sow good, not evil. You can't control their harvest, but you can manage yours.

WHAT LOVE IS

CHAPTER 9:
LOVE IS PATIENT

Be joyful in hope, patient in affliction,
faithful in prayer. -Romans 12:12

THERE IS JUST SOMETHING ABOUT WAITING IN LINES that will bring out the best or worst in us. Waiting will expose the true character of a person. Want to know the stuff you're made of? Pay attention to how you respond to waiting in lines. Whether it's a road traffic jam or standing in a grocery line, you will learn a lot about yourself and the strength of your patience in how you wait. What do you do when you're waiting? How do you respond? Do you wait in serenity? Or do you get frustrated or angry? Do you strike out at others for holding up your mission? And why do you respond in the way you do? Where are you going anyhow? And was the cost of ripping someone else up in the process worth the rush?

Quick fixes aren't the answer. Your growth is the answer. Yet, it's easy to get caught up in the hype of instant gratification when you're surrounded by a hurried way of living. Some of us are all too familiar with Veruca Salt's version of "I Want It Now" from the movie *Willy Wonka and the Chocolate Factory*. Not only do you know the words by heart, but you continue to sing that same song subconsciously, even now.

I really considered myself to be a patient person until God took me to new levels in patience. I know full well about being careful what to ask for, as there were things I didn't realize I was asking of God or simply wasn't clear on or specific about my petitions (smiling). So now, I really try to understand what I'm really asking from God. In my prayers, I try not to ask God to send things for which to be patient, but I ask God to give me the patience for the things He's trying to make great in my life. So, why am I surprised when He's making things great and placing yet another development challenge in my path? Through it all, the blessing is that I am really learning how to rest. When He's in high gear, so are my opportunities for growth, and when He's at rest, I know I get to enjoy the fruits of His labor. There He is again, trying to make it great, so let me step aside and allow Him to work His masterpiece.

Patient love endures and doesn't give up easily. It sees possibility over incapability. It sees you at your worst, yet it knows that with its power, you'll be at your best. It cheers you on to completion. It knows you're worth the wait. It meets you where you are and comes through with flying colors. It is committed. It speaks words of encouragement...words that build up rather than tear down. It's gentle. It is true. It perseveres and actively prepares for the ultimate expression of itself. It doesn't hurt. It knows and understands. It's faithful. It waits lovingly. It's beautiful. It trusts. It's at peace and calm. Patient love stands the test of time! It gives you the space to figure it out but prays for you along the journey. Its love trumps the impossible. Its love is truly enough. Patient love doesn't fight against but fights for forever.

Know What You Want

Know what you want and be willing to wait for it. Anything of greatness requires time; greatness is a process that requires persistence to see worthy results. Delicious cuisine is one where I'm pretty clear about what I want and am willing to wait for its greatness. I love food! I mean, I really love food! But I can be picky about what

I eat. I like really good food, but I like it most when wrapped with lots of love. Over the last few years, "gooey butter cake" has become my dessert of choice. My cousin, who is an executive chef, makes the most amazingly rich gooey butter cake, so whenever he can make it for me, that's what I'm partaking in. To get it to the perfection he does, there is an involved process, and you must be patient for its finish.

Most often in relationships, people want "stellar," yet to get stellar you must be patient. People may come close to everything you want but likely won't be everything you want. However, we must allow patience to make them complete in Him. Settling says, "You're taking too long, so I'm just going to go right on ahead and pick somebody. Somebody is better than nobody." Then, later, you're all in an uproar because you took the cake out of the oven too soon. When you cut into it and found out it was uncooked on the inside, you were thoroughly disappointed. Instead of putting the cake back in the oven and waiting until it's finished, you throw it away. The funny thing about impatience is that whether you make a new cake or put the existing one back in the oven, you still have to wait. There is just no getting around it. So choose how you will wait. Wait anxious and hurried or at peace and trusting. I don't know about you, but I've had my share of anxious and hurried; and I'll wait in tranquility and take my slice of greatness when it's done, thank you!

A Picture of Patience

It was a spring evening, and I had stolen away from the after-work traffic to one of my newest hideaways to get some writing done. This chic, Indian-style restaurant, in Upper Kirby, served a butter chicken and sayel lamb that I couldn't wait to taste. When the curly haired server asked for my order, there was no hesitation that it would be the usual Rancher Thalis, but this time with sautéed greens as a replacement side.

I took in the subtle breeze on the patio. As I basked in the settling evening sun, a fair-skinned mother with a short haircut that fashioned her small face walked by with three full-of-life young girls. If I had to guess, I would say they had to be between ages seven and nine. They were lovely, well-mannered young ladies. Two of them appeared to be sisters while the other young girl a family friend. I couldn't help but to notice their engagement as they sat next to my table on the Pondicheri patio. Before they could sit down, I heard one young girl ask, "Can we watch *Blackish* when we get home?" The loving mother, without reservation, gave them the okay for a date with the Johnson family. The mother hyped the girls up about the mango lassi. When one asked what it was, the mother said, "Well, we're just going to order one for each of you so you can taste." She assured them they'd love it. Here I was sitting next to these inquisitive minds, and I too was starting to consider adding a lassi of my own to my tab.

You could see the mother had had a long day and could have imagined herself on that patio alone with her feet propped and enjoying a quiet glass of peace. However, she chose to be present without a cell phone or other distractions to occupy her time. During dinner, they played games at the table. They would each describe themselves as an animal or a thing that the others had to guess what it was. I heard the mother say, "I'm gray with a hole in the top of my head." Before she could finish her description, one girl shouted, "A whale!" I smiled and chuckled inside as the mother seemed somewhat disappointed that she got the answer so fast, but was happy all at the same time. They were enjoying themselves, and there just seemed to be a lot of love at that table. And I was really enjoying them, too. I admired the mother for her patience and for the priceless investment of connection she was making with these young girls. When one of the girls spilled her drink, the mother handled it with grace—there was no yelling, but a very loving "It's okay; stuff happens" kind of spirit. Above all, she just had their best interest at heart.

The thing about patience is that you don't always get to see its fruit in the here and now, but one day you will. There were so many small teachings at that table that will have a major impact on the young girls and their own families someday.

As they headed for home, I noticed the time, and I too decided to scurry home...*Blackish* was about to come on!

Love in Action: Patience

1. Pray that God will show you how to trust Him with your relationships and strengthen your faith during your seasons of waiting for Him to make you and/or your relationships greater.

2. Carve out some quiet time each week to do absolutely nothing but be still and listen. Even if it's just for fifteen minutes, start with something and continue to build upon your quiet time. Soon, you'll be a pro at resting!

3. Gift someone with your undivided attention; make a conscious effort to be present for one whole hour. Do not pick up your phone (even if they do). Don't check any social media, turn on the TV, or look out the window. What did you experience?

CHAPTER 10:
LOVE IS KIND

Be kind and compassionate to one another, forgiving each other, just as in Christ God forgave you. -Ephesians 4:32

EVERY DECISION HAS AN ACTION, AND EVERY ACTION has a reaction. Kindness is contagious. It is the very essence of goodness and mercy. It gives even when others may have proven themselves undeserving. Therefore, it is very hard to keep up a spirit of meanness when someone is always being kind to you. If you remain in its presence long enough, you will eventually find yourself being drawn to its beauty and transformed by its kind of love.

If you have ever found yourself drawn to a loving person, it is likely that they are also kind. There is just something about the spirit of kindness that breathes an overwhelming air of love. Kind people have a way of bringing a calmness and joy to your being because you know they love you through compassion. They are genuinely warm and have no hidden agendas with their love. They simply just want to love.

Nonetheless, don't mistake kindness with passivity, going along to get along, or a need to please others. When you're choosing to do something for others, check your motives. There are so many other things in disguise perpetrating to be kindness. Ask yourself, "Why am I doing this?" Is it an avenue to get someone to respond to you in a certain way or a need to receive something in return? If so, it's quite certain it isn't love.

The best way to know that it is love in kindness is when you have done something for someone and have no need whatsoever to receive anything for it...not from the person you gave to or from anyone else. That means you don't remind the person of an act of kindness you shared with them when you feel like you're not getting what you want out of the relationship. It means you don't make your giving a newsflash to receive a pat on the back. It means you don't look for famed accolades for your efforts or expect to receive something from the world for what you did for someone. As hard as this can be sometimes, even if a person doesn't say thank you, still be kind. Don't change the heart of who you are because of someone else. When I visited China, my Beijing tour guide said it best: "Don't let other people's mistakes punish you."

I love giving gifts. I love seeing people smile. Yet, for me, it is the smallest kindnesses that show great love. The night of my thirtieth birthday celebration, a friend and "little sister" from college surprised me with the sweetest kindness. In the midst of my party, my little sister pulled me aside and simply poured into me the warmest words of positivity. She shared with me how she had admired me in college and how I had inspired her and impacted her life. I was completely overcome by her love!

Still to this day, I remember that moment; and water puddles well up in these brown eyes every time I attempt to share that memory with someone...even now. It was the greatest act of kindness. She didn't want anything but to share her love for me and to see me at my best that night and always. A year later, she and her fiancé (also a good friend of mine) would pay me another act of kindness when they married and asked me to cater their rehearsal dinner. They explained how they had privately discussed supporting me in my business venture and that it was important to them that I be a part of their marriage celebration. They entrusted me with all of the details of the dinner. I can remember asking about aspects of the menu to the décor and her responding with, "We're focused on the marriage, not the wedding." It was the greatest honor to serve a couple on their special day who embodied such pure hearts and one of the highest acts of kindness I'd received.

Kindness Is a Strength

People often see kindness as a weakness. However, it takes strength to be loving to a world that can be so cruel. Kindness is truth bound by tenderness and consideration. To love kindly means to love with care; I care about you as a person and your well-being. A kind heart wants you to experience all that is good and positive at its utmost. It receives joy in seeing you glowing, happy, and thriving. Yet, it will not withhold opportunities for growth in your life at the fear of hurting your feelings because it wants so much to see you at your best always. Kind love says, "I love you enough to give you an honest and fair assessment with a great deal of care."

However, to truly know kindness, you must be able to give and receive it. You cannot love without giving, so if you have a kind heart, it's likely you're often trying to take care of others before you take care of yourself. Whatever you're always doing for others may just be the thing you need to learn to do for yourself.

Before the departure of every flight, the flight attendant comes over the airways to provide you with a safety briefing and remind you of the FAA flight regulations. Passengers who are traveling with children are advised to secure their own oxygen mask first before assisting with children. Why? If you attempt to secure everyone else's mask before you do your own, it's likely you will not only fail at saving them, but you also won't even have enough breath in your body to save yourself. You are more likely to be effective at saving others when you can first breathe. Then, and only then, do you have the capacity to help others. This is your flight attendant speaking, and I am reminding you to be kind to yourself…secure your oxygen mask first.

Kindness Doesn't Discriminate

Kindness doesn't discriminate. To be kind to those who are kind to you goes without saying. The work and growth come from being kind to those who are not very nice. When someone says or does something to you (or rather to someone you love) that is mean or cruel, it can become second nature for so many to want to see the same harm done in return. Yet, Matthew 6:15 declares, "But if you do not forgive men their sins, your Father will not forgive your sins." As much as you may want to shake them real good, kill them instead with kindness.

Ciarra was in the second grade when she crossed paths with Grace. Grace had made it very clear that she didn't like Ciarra. At every turn, she would find a way to be mean or rude to Ciarra. She would give Ciarra intimidating looks that could destroy a person. Because Grace didn't like her, Ciarra had concluded that she didn't like Grace either.

One day, Ciarra spoke with her mom about the girl at school. Stacie, her mom, told Ciarra that no matter how mean Grace was to her, she should always be nice, loving, and kind. She shared with her daughter, "You need to be Jesus with skin on." She further explained to Ciarra that some people don't know how to be a friend because no one has been a friend to them. Ciarra took heed to her mother's words and chose to be just that. She thought that if she showed Grace love through kindness, then she could see that they could someday be friends. Well, to her surprise, eventually the kindness that Ciarra showed Grace worked! Grace began to warm to Ciarra, and they grew to be really good friends. When the kids had to present a story at school on who was their hero, Grace chose Ciarra. Grace shared that Ciarra was her hero because no matter how mean or rude she was to her, she was always kind. It took a loving mother to teach her daughter a lesson on how to love. And it took an obedient daughter to give that love away. Ciarra's mother wanted her to learn that you never know what an act of kindness can do for someone or who may be watching. Now in the seventh grade, both Ciarra and Grace are forever changed by that gift of kindness.

Love in Action: Kindness

1. Pray God's best for someone who has wronged you. Ask God to allow you to see and respond to the person from His perspective. Most importantly, have compassion and forgive him or her.

2. Take out thirty minutes today to do something kind for yourself and put on your oxygen mask first.

3. Gift someone with a random act of kindness today. Volunteer to babysit for that loved one who clearly needs a break. Pay someone a compliment. Pay for the meal of the person who sits alone at the restaurant. Do not share with anyone what you did for the other person and expect nothing in return. Watch God smile!

CHAPTER 11:
LOVE REJOICES WITH THE TRUTH

An honest answer is like a kiss on the lips. -Proverbs 24:26

THE SOURCE OF ALL TRUTH HAS BEEN WRITTEN. THE knowledge of good versus evil, love versus hate, and conditional versus unconditional has all been written. However, so many people in the world have revised or dismissed the truth of God's word. We have instead twisted His word or decided to create our own truth. We then live out that version of the truth and slap God's name on it, or have the boldness to call it authentic. God created the law not to limit or restrict us but to give us freedom. He did it to protect us from enslavement. If you look at every law or commandment from the time He spoke with Eve in the garden about not eating from the "tree of the knowledge of good and evil" to the creation of the Holy Spirit-inspired book we know as the Bible, He had a plan of protection for each of us. We step outside of His perfect will of protection when we choose to operate in disobedience to what He says is good for us. When we refuse to accept His truth or reject His original design, what we experience is no longer His perfect will but His permissive will (Matthew 19:8).

The Wounds of a Friend

Have a "rock" team, those who keep you grounded and speak truth into your life. Surround yourself with those who don't just tell you what you want to hear, but give you an honest account of yourself, yet say it with so much love that you want to embrace the needed change(s).

We say we want to know the truth, but do we really? When those around us tell us what we want to hear, everything is wonderful, but the moment someone shares some constructive criticism, we get all tied up in a knot. Sometimes the constructive feedback will have us running in the opposite direction if we're not open to what they have to say. If they are not careful, we may even cut ties and never allow ourselves to hear some version of the truth ever again. We write it off as they're getting too comfortable or that they know nothing about us. And that may be true to some extent, but have you stopped to consider that there indeed may be some truth in what they are presenting, at least from their perspective?

Get comfortable with the intimacy of the truth. If you embrace it, the truth can be utterly freeing. The truth isn't always a delight to hear, at least not initially, but it's a love you learn to appreciate in the long run. The truth can be a challenge to share with those we love, but if you really care about your loved one, you will share the truth. The truth is not ridicule or criticism masqueraded as love, but it does ask the hard questions in an attempt to understand. It has evaluated the entire landscape and is able to give a good assessment of what's true. If you're not able to come to a point in your relationship where truth can be shared, it will reside in shallow waters and never know depth. If you can't share truth, do you really love and care about that person the way you claim you do? I'm a person who has always hated to be the bearer of bad news...at least what appears to be bad news. Yet, I've learned that if I really care about a person, it's best to brave potential opposition over silent comfort. And when a person knows your heart and your desire for their good, they will eventually come to a place of appreciation for your looking out for them.

If you truly love someone, you want to see them succeed, even if that success isn't in your own life. You will want to see them profit from your mistakes and not have to endure the same challenges or perceived failures. You won't validate their feelings to allow them to continue to do less than their best. You won't care if they hate you in the short-term for trying to warn them of foreseeable dangers ahead. You will lovingly share without fear areas in which they can grow and mature.

Be Honest with Yourself

Partial disobedience is complete disobedience. Don't be mistaken by what you perceive as a small error to be absent of sin. Be true to yourself. Disobedience is likened to keep putting your hand on a hot stove and not expecting to get burned. When we disobey God, we commit spiritual adultery. Don't allow denial to cause you to believe otherwise, or your biggest teacher will be that thing that brings you to your knees.

I truly believe that when you know better, most times you will choose to do better. Though, when God has presented you with His word and wise counsel in the flesh, yet you're still wandering around in the desert, you may be enabling versus choosing wisely. It could be that you're opting to be defiant. It may be you who He's waiting on to come to a place of truth versus you waiting on His great reveal.

At times, you can want something so badly that you're trying to fit a square peg into a round hole, and it's more than obvious it doesn't fit. There is nothing wrong with the square peg as there is nothing wrong with a round hole. Both would be served best, however, with a square hole and a round peg, respectively. When you're honest with yourself, the difference is clear.

Depending on how it's delivered, the truth can be a delight. Have integrity, and tell the truth. It may hurt them, but you hurt them more by not allowing a person to know what is real and true. We can be real but wrong in our candor, so give the truth with the kindest delivery you know. Know that it's not your decision to withhold the facts or share only part of the picture. Withholding key information robs another of free will. Even our Father in Heaven doesn't do that for anyone. You honor God best when you honor the free will of His people.

Love in Action: Truth

1. Petition God for forgiveness for a time when you chose to lie instead of trusting Him with telling the truth. Ask God for His truth and for Him to show you how to live by that truth.

2. Be honest, even when you have no audience. What is your vice of dishonesty? Choose integrity in that area of your life.

3. The next time you're presented with constructive feedback, choose to listen and consider the perspective. Resist the urge to cut them off and allow them to share their complete thoughts rather than debate that their feedback is refutable. Instead, wait for the person to finish, respond with positive receipt of the information, and give thanks for the courage to share. Believe that they have your best interest at heart and are not seeking to destroy you.

4. Where it is absolutely necessary, find the courage to share an honest account with someone you claim you love. Seek prayer before approaching him or her. Make sure the truth is given with lots of love and not masked with a need to be right.

CHAPTER 12:
LOVE ALWAYS PROTECTS

*No weapon that is formed against thee shall
prosper. -Isaiah 54:17 (KJV)*

CHOOSE WHO WILL SIT AT YOUR TABLE. BE DISCERNING about who will stand with you in your promise to love. Protection in your relationships starts with your choices and selection of confidants, with God being the number one confidant. In relationships, it's each of your responsibilities to protect the heart of the other, but it's also your responsibility to protect your own heart by choosing someone who is a good match for you. That goes for all relationships. Protect with the words you speak so as not to harm. Protect with your fidelity and honesty. Protect with your prayers. Protect with commitment.

Love Protects the Unity of Your Relationships

Your relationships will be tested. If your devotion is founded upon shallow streams of emotional feelings or lust rather than the deep depths of unconditional love and acceptance, it will risk breakage. One of your best measures of protection will be your beginnings; start your relationships with a solid foundation of empathy and intimacy. More importantly, start your relationships by entrusting it to God's design and leading.

Within the marital relationship, God established that the woman is the rib (protection of his heart and aid in his breathing) of the man. They are one flesh. His word says "thou shall leave and cleave" (Genesis 2:24). Not only was this intended to institute you as one flesh, but it was to protect your newly formed union as well. God needed you to have the freedom to define your own path and legacy.

Protect the unity of your relationships by not allowing yourself or others to tear it apart. If you stand together as one, your bond will be unbreakable. Don't allow others to come in the middle of your relationship, not even you. You break your bond when you start thinking only of yourself and choose to stand alone. You may have differences with your spouse or closest confidant but never let anyone bring any gossip or division between the two of you. No parents, in-laws, children, friends, or foe will be able to weaken your union if you don't give them the green light to do so. You contribute to the demise of your own relationships when you invite others in by exposing intimate details and trusts.

Love Protects the Name and Reputation of Others

You protect others by blessing their good name and reputation. There is nothing more beautiful than being able to be completely vulnerable with another person and that person upholding your confidence with the upmost protection. Love protects the best interest of others.

Love doesn't seek to annihilate. What good could possibly come from trying to ruin the life of another? What does it say about you as a person who seeks to spread a rumor? Love protects the virtue of others. It protects their reputation by always speaking well of them. It esteems and gives credibility. Even when good isn't spoken about a person, love will find a way to still honor them in the midst of malice gossip or hate. Equally, in truth, it will still honor others by focusing on what's good about them and not what's still under construction. It will question those that seek to lay slander on them. When others try to start a fire of gossip, love will pour cold water on the fire. Even if the information is true, what you speak about others says more about your character than the character of the person you speak of.

Love Protects Others from Harm

Love knows that hurting others is not just about physical harm but it knows you can hurt with your words. No matter what we were taught as children, our words can harm. Love won't harm with an intent to hurt. Our words hold power, and love is careful about the words it speaks because it knows it can break the spirits of another.

When I think of protecting others, I think about what's for their good. Love that protects wants to keep you from getting hurt. Be clear that it's not the selfish type of love that protects itself by deception: omitting key information, telling half-truths, or simply not telling everything. Love doesn't lie, cheat, or ask others to lie for it. It doesn't put you in compromising situations that may have negative, lasting impacts. It doesn't put you in danger or ask for ill hook-ups. It doesn't place you in high-risk situations that may be life-threatening.

In the age of reality TV and social media, more and more relationships are getting devalued and watered down. Instead of using these mediums for good, the cowards and bullies have established themselves by throwing stones and hiding. They use these forums to tell others what they really think about them, and what they think is often not very positive. The spectators stand in awe and watch to see who is going to take the next punch. We applaud the brave of heart, those who are able to give the best argument and be the last man or woman standing. It's become pure entertainment to see others being torn down. Rarely are others standing in the gap to say, "This isn't right." However, real love doesn't care about the perceived win; it cares about the relationship. It cares about the heart and health of the person. It doesn't delight in hurting those we claim to love or not love.

Take a stand for someone. Find a cause that serves the well-being of others. Be a voice or refuge for an individual who needs your protection. When you see someone being mistreated, take a risk (smart risk) to be the shield he or she may need.

Love Protects Through Prayer

Prayer covers a magnitude of sins. One of the highest compliments you can pay someone is to cover them in prayer. I'm thankful for the many prayers, from my grandparents to complete strangers, that have been sent up on my behalf and for my good. God protects and guides your every step. If you don't already thank Him enough, I'm sure you'd thank Him more often if you only knew the dangers you were in and what He saved you from each and every day.

As a young girl, I can remember one night stopping in the kitchen just before turning in for bed. My mother and brother were already fast asleep, and my father was at work. As I stood in the kitchen, I could see the door knob turning on the kitchen door that connected to the garage. The deadbolt was locked but that lock on the knob clearly was not. For a moment, I wondered if it was my father coming home early, but something in my gut told me that it was not him. Instead of waking my mother or calling the police, I, for whatever reason, went to my room and prayed to God that whoever was on the other side of that door would go away. The next morning, I shared with my mother what I had experienced the night before. When my mother checked everything out, the external garage door was clearly unlocked as was the kitchen doorknob, but none of us was harmed and nothing was taken. Yet for years, I had nightmares about who was on the other side of that door until I went away to college.

Later in my adulthood, I encountered a similar situation while housesitting for a relative who was away on business. I decided to leave work early that day so I could beat traffic and get by the house to check on everything before heading home. To my surprise there was a major wreck on the freeway and the longest detour I had ever experienced. By the time I arrived at my relative's home, I was a bit worn. I kept having problems getting the key to work in the door, so by the time I got the door open, the alarm was sounding. I thought I had done something to trigger the alarm and went to the keypad to cancel the alert to the security provider. Then there was this complete silence, and I could hear cars driving by on the main road as if a window was open. I found myself being drawn to this still sound until it led me to the back of the house where I found the kitchen door lying on the dining room table. At the ability to snap out of my trance, I resorted to exit the house and take safety. This time, I called the police, as I wasn't certain if the perpetrator was in the house. While waiting for the police to arrive, I contacted the security provider. I asked them what time the back door was triggered, and the time given was one minute before my entrance to the front door. I was again unharmed, and nothing was taken.

The enemy can see the plan and relationships God has for your life and will use whatever he can to try to destroy them. He knew how many nights I had wrestled in my sleep from the first attempt. Unlike our Heavenly Father, he has the same tricks and is quite predictable. Of course, he would try to use the same tactic again the second time around to harm me, but unfortunately for him, it just made me stronger. "You intended to harm me, but God intended it for good to accomplish what is now being done, the saving of many lives" (Genesis 50:20).

When love sees trouble down the road on the left, it will encourage you to take the path to the right. Yet, it knows that by free will it can't protect you at every turn and knows that some paths you just have to take for yourself. Know that those detoured paths are always within healthy realms of strengthening and work together for your good. God was protecting me through the long detours to strengthen my trust in Him and His plans for my life. So, whoever is on the other side of your door trying to harm you or your relationships, pray that they'll go away.

Love in Action: Protection

1. Pray that God will protect you from hurt, harm, and danger as well as be a fence of protection for those you know, and for the world in general.

2. Participate in your own protection by seeking to make good, wise decisions. Own your choices.

3. Protect the name of those whom you know and even those you don't know. Keep a confidence that was entrusted to you by not exposing another's private matters.

CHAPTER 13:
LOVE ALWAYS TRUSTS

Trust in the Lord with all your heart and lean not on your own understanding; in all your ways acknowledge Him, and He will make your paths straight. -Proverbs 3:5–6

YOU CAN BE SKEPTICAL OF THE WRONG PEOPLE because of where you've spent your time. That reliance on distrust will keep you from experiencing a deep connection with those who truly have your back. To build trust, you must be willing to surrender the belief that he or she has ill intentions, specifically when he or she hasn't given you a reason to think otherwise. The best security is the ability to accept uncertainty. The mind is most of the battle.

I was reminded of a matter of trust one morning as I prepared for my drive to a place I had never been. When I entered the destination in my cell phone, Maps told me to go one way. Once I changed positions and got to the main street, it told me to go a different way. I was TEMPTED to go by the initial directions, but I decided to submit to the new route. What I learned is that the old way would have taken me longer to get there. God will, at times, switch the plan based on your position (readiness). Don't delay your blessings by trying to take the old way. Learn to trust His instruction!

Trusting God

God never broke a promise. When He committed, He did it with great zeal. The most amazing artistic expression of God's love through promise was His creation of the rainbow. In all its splendor, the beauty and tranquility it renders is unmatched. When I see a rainbow, I'm reminded of all of God's miracles and who is really in control.

Love for God is expressed in our obedience and trust in Him. If you don't trust Him, you'll have a hard time trusting period. When you're able to give your life to God, then and only then can you begin to love others. Practically all references in the Bible point to trust in God, not in man. God commanded that we are to love others, but trust was His responsibility. Trusting in God requires complete submission to Him and Him alone.

Love is trust. Trust is faith taken to the next level. It is merely a greater confidence and assurance of hope. Faith is not asking God to show you a miracle to prove Himself to you. If He has to prove Himself, it's not trusting Him. At such a request, I'm sure He's like, "Wasn't my dying on the cross enough? How many Red Sea partings and feedings must I perform for you to believe?" God wants you to be clear about the source of your refuge with great assurance. He needs you to understand that those you love will error but that He requires you to love them anyhow.

If you want something more than God, it could be an idol. God may test you in the desires of your heart by removing that thing that means the most to you. What will your love say then? Will you respond as Abraham did (Genesis 22:1–19) or like the two-faced prostitute (1 Kings 3:16–28)?

There Is Beauty in Your Flaws

If you're critical of yourself and beat yourself up when you make mistakes, you'll do the same to others. Be kind to yourself. Allow yourself to have flaws. There is beauty in flaws too! If you try to hide your flaws, you will love with walls erected.

Just as blessings come back to us full circle, we all have to share in some aspect of hurt or grief. What distinguishes the great is that they learn to trust in the midst of their circumstances. Those who erect walls to prevent anyone else from getting to their hearts must be careful that they are not designing their own loneliness. Whatever fear or hurt you're holding on to, I am asking you to open your hand and release it. Give it to the One who can change your darkness into sunshine. I don't want you to hurt anymore. Yet the more you hold on to it, the more it's going to pierce every fiber of your being. I want you to be free to love. I want you to be fearless in your love, because love knows not fear. "There is no fear in love. But perfect love drives out fear, because fear has to do with punishment. The one who fears is not made perfect in love" (1 John 4:18).

Your Past Is Not Your Present

Distrust is often a result of never knowing the ability to trust. Perhaps someone robbed you of the choice to trust or took advantage of your vulnerability so now you don't trust anyone, not even your ability to make good choices. When trust is broken, it can be very hard to regain it. Yet, the regaining of trust flows into other relationships.

We have all had our hearts broken at some point or another. I don't know anyone who hasn't experienced a loss or hurt of some kind. Pain is inevitable. But that doesn't mean you did anything wrong or that God is punishing you. If you're experiencing pain, it's likely you're being conditioned for something greater.

Believe the best for your relationships. You need to remember that the man or woman in front of you is not those behind you. You need to give him or her the due respect you would want without fear, and believe that he or she is not out to get you unless he or she exemplifies that. Don't overanalyze the relationship and consider that all is well. When criticism is presented, take the time to let the person know your sentiments on criticism versus encouragement or positive affirmation without being snappy. When people don't seek to understand, help them to understand…that's just part of the work of the communication that is necessary for a healthy relationship.

Trusting by Letting Go

Letting go requires trust. Trust that God knows best and is more than capable to give each of us exactly what we need without waver. When we don't let go, we are saying, "But God, don't you see what I see. Surely, I know better than you!"

Sometimes we have this nervous, tight grip on life, but the thing about such a firm grasp is that nothing can flow in or out. It may be best to just let go and enjoy the journey and trust God. He doesn't need us not trusting Him. All worry is the inability to give it all to Him and trust Him. Worry steals life away, not to mention what it does to your health. God can't birth what He's trying to bless you with in an environment of distrust.

Those whom we love will hurt us even when they don't intend to. No one is perfect, and all will make mistakes that impact you. But what are you going to do about it? You are the leading man or leading lady in your own story whether you realize it or not. There is more for your life if you simply unwrap the gift and allow yourself to love and be loved. Trust that God knows what He is doing and stop being a backseat driver; just enjoy the ride. It's hard to enjoy the ride when you're constantly doing all the choosing versus allowing God to orchestrate the blessing.

One of my close cousins flew in one winter weekend to hang out with me. Being the gentleman he is, he insisted on driving me around so I could relax for a change; so, I gave him the keys to my car. At first, it was a bit of a challenge trusting him to drive and handle my ride with the care I would. When I concluded that he had my best interest at heart and was an experienced driver, I began to let go of the need to tell him how to operate my vehicle. As I sat back and let go, the drive became more enjoyable and fun. From that point on, every time we got to the car, there was this peace of contentment, and I was happy to give him the keys. When I didn't trust, I was tense and probably not making the ride enjoyable for him either. Letting go and trusting was a far better and relaxing choice.

Trust in the Good

Trusting means you get rid of the habit of always assuming the worst. The reality of your ability to trust just may be a product of your own belief. Take an examination of your thoughts and conversation. Listen to what you speak into your own life. No one has the power to hurt you more than yourself. Your lack of trust will be laced in negativity. It will poison your belief. You will come up with every excuse as to why you shouldn't do something. Choose to fast on the negativity.

I love it when God surprises people in spite of their distrust with a new awakening. That moment when all the negative things that were spoken but God says, "That's not true; you're looking at this all wrong." Then, BAM! That same person or experience they were speaking so negatively about does something so surprisingly nice out of the blue. I just LOVE it when that happens! I can't say, "See, I told you," so I just smile.

Believing for the good doesn't mean you ignore the godly discernment you were gifted with, but it encourages you to not overanalyze stuff or create things that are simply not there. Even though he or she may not get it right at times in your eyes, trust they are not conspiring to harm you. There is humility of heart when someone says, "I'm sorry; I hurt you," and you know they mean it. Do that for those you love.

God says to lean not on your own understanding. We mess it up when we try to understand a divine plan with human logic. Trust in God. Faith is not knowing what the end will be, but knowing that the end will be His absolute best divine plan for you. It's less about a fixation on the absolute and more about the belief in the beauty of the abstract of His creation. Even when we don't have all the answers and choose to rest anyhow, He will show you the power of His peace in the midst of all the unknowns. Take courage in knowing He has your back!

Love in Action: Trust

1. Pray and ask God to show you how to put your trust in Him above all others and allow Him to do His best work. Forgive those who you trusted but defiled your trust. Ask God for the wisdom and discernment to make better choices.

2. Believe that you have the power to make great decisions. Learn to listen to (not ignore) that inner voice that tells you this is not the best way...that way is best.

3. Open your heart to allow love to flow through you to others. Give someone the benefit of the doubt when they have given you no reason to distrust otherwise.

CHAPTER 14:
LOVE ALWAYS HOPES

For I know the plans I have for you, declares the Lord,
plans to prosper you and not to harm you, plans to
give you hope and a future. -Jeremiah 29:11

THE MIND IS A POWERFUL THING. YOU CAN'T GO beyond what you don't believe. Faith is believing that although there is no evidence that lends itself to the possibility, it elects to trust it can happen anyhow, despite what it sees. It is the choosing to focus on the positive instead of the negative; it is a decision to settle in on the belief, not the unbelief. Hope is not desperation nor is it foolish. It believes for God's greatest yet functions within the boundaries of God's will. Hope is the charge in your lifeline. It takes courage and focuses on the promises. It dwells in expectancy. When you hope, you begin to live out that very thing you've been expecting. The miracles come when you believe.

After traveling over twenty-four hours, we had safely arrived to Durban, South Africa, from Dallas, Texas. Our Concord Church Missions team, weary, was in fact ready for a good night's rest. As we settled into our respective hotel rooms and turned on the television, there on the news was word about the death of former President

Nelson Mandela. On December 5, 2013, we had stepped into the motherland on the night of one of the most pivotal times in our history; the days to follow would be a moment in time that none of us would forget.

The next morning, we arose to serve at an orphanage nearby. Through the eyes of these children, you could see their pain. But their voices were the most beautiful things I had ever heard...pain and sorrow, joy and strength all wrapped in one song. They were more than survivors; they were my heroes. Treasured hearts so pure awaiting for a love to come along, for they were orphans as we know it in the sense of the word, but they were also one big family that loved and supported one another. I fell in love with my sassy, dark-skin chile. Her heart was so pure, yet her spirit was so colorful. She would light up a room, and her dance was solid rhythm. She was courageous even with her mud-stained hands and feet. We all fought for a moment to hold her in our arms and get one of those adorable kisses she bore. As Lauryn Hill would say, it was the sweetest thing I've ever known. I would have put her on the next plane with me if legalities would have permitted me to do so.

They were all so amazing. Yet, despite their impoverished surroundings and barren land, they hoped. In the immediate, things could have looked dim, but if you sat still for a moment to take in the beautiful horizon, you knew there was something out there waiting to receive the gift these young faces had to offer to the world. And hope came along and replaced soiled mattresses with new clean ones. Total room makeovers were done with new comforter sets and curtains. Their pantries became stocked. Each child was fitted for a new pair of shoes thanks to Buckner Shoes for Orphan Souls. We planted a vegetable garden with some of every vegetable for the taking. Donations were used to replace their water cisterns. Their playground was of old tires and wooden swings that hung from tree limbs and one slide for all the kids to share. At the top of the hill where their house sat, the view was breathtaking. Next to the house was a pile of bricks that sat in the yard as a dream deferred. Yet in their native tongue and American English, they sang, "You are faithful, O Lord; you are faithful, O Lord, every day and every hour you are faithful, O Lord."

Nights later, the rain beat against the night sky, and the swirls of wind felt like it would have taken us by storm. Our room flooded; we gathered ourselves and retreated to safe haven. Earlier that morning, we were awoken to clouds, drizzle, and mist. We were certain the clinical need would be scarce, as we had served at least 150 patients in Bizana the day prior when the sun was bright and air was dry. With the storm still on the cusp, we knew for sure we'd be back early on this day and thought those villagers living nearby would have retreated to their dry coverings and enjoyed some peace and rest.

As we drove down the dirt road, there were more people out than I would have expected. They were walking down the side of the road with their umbrellas gathered as if they were on a mission that couldn't be missed. When we arrived again at the unfinished concrete church, there was a double line that extended beyond the front entrance. The word had spread throughout the village about those patients we had served the day before. Despite the dismal outlook in the sky, these natives of Bizana came with hope. My heart was full at the sight.

Although I saw no promise in the sky, I saw promise in their hearts. As I sat at the registration table, they came one by one with not just one ailment but multiple. I had a translator to help me complete the required forms for triage. One of the fields on the form was "Responsible Person." My fair lady, who sat across from me at the registration table, wrote "Jesus" in that space. I was blown away by the faith of these people, how they could worship and praise God literally for hours. They rested in Him; they believed in Him and had immeasurable faith. We run through church in the States like an hour or two infringes upon our priorities. But they praise all day, and I'm sure every chance they get. I could see the spirit of our ancestors being passed through their tradition of worship. It's the songs that gave our enslaved forefathers the hope to make it through one of the difficult seasons of the African American history. I admired their adoration for our Heavenly Father. We covered them in prayer, and they graciously received the blessings.

By the end of the clinic, we had served well over four hundred patients although we had only planned meds for two hundred. We celebrated God's provision through song and dance. We had come from America to serve Winnie's people and to give to them, but it was we, I believe, who were blessed more. They cooked for us, and as I peeked through the kitchen admiring one chef to another, it was clear the food was full of love. Just prior to our departure, the mothers of the village sat us down as if we were royalty and draped us one by one with fine handmade gifts of jewelry. I received a purple and green beaded bracelet that I continue to cherish today. The teachings of their culture, prayers, deeds, and everything they showed us despite their humble surroundings will be forever etched in my heart and spirit! It is always a joy and an honor to experience God in new and exciting ways! As we drove away, I had mixed emotions…I wanted to stay to do more, but I knew we still had others to serve along our journey. I had met five little boys, my little buddies, who had made an indelible impression upon me and kept my heart smiling. It seemed they followed me everywhere during those two days of the clinic. And at our departure, I regrettably watched my little buddies chase our van down the road while waving cheerful good-byes. Their faces were aglow, and their smiles of joy would have melted your heart and filled your cup all in one breath.

When the outlook in your relationship is full of high rains, gather your umbrella and step out into the rain. Weather it like you have a mission that can't be missed. Have hope.

Love in Action: Hope

1. Pray to God for His plans for your life and align your desires and will according to those plans. Ask God to give you renewed hope where you have replaced it with disbelief. Pray that He would strengthen your faith in those areas where you struggle the most.

2. Create a vision for your future based on what you believe God wants for your life. Write that vision down in word and/or pictorial form, whichever is your preference. Believe it will happen.

3. Be a source of encouragement for someone struggling with belief in a better future. Send them a scripture that serves their current circumstance or a note or card of inspiration that uplifts their spirit.

CHAPTER 15:
LOVE ALWAYS PERSEVERES

Consider it pure joy, my brothers, whenever you face trials of many kinds, because you know that the testing of your faith develops perseverance. Perseverance must finish its work so that you may be mature and complete, not lacking anything. -James 1:2–4

YOU ARE NOT A QUITTER. THE MIDDLE OF THE TUNNEL is always the darkest. When you're experiencing your darkest days, it doesn't mean that you have reached the end; it just means you haven't reached the other side…your destiny. There is always light at the end of the tunnel. Focus on that.

"To have and to hold from this day forward, for better, for worse, for richer, for poorer, in sickness and health, until death do us part." This is what God had in mind when He established marriage. Whether in private commitment or public vow, you gave someone your word that you would forever stand by their side. To have a ride-or-die in your life (be it a spouse, friend, relative, associate, or neighbor) is the best kind of blessing. The sun won't always shine bright, and the cold nights won't always pass with a shared blanket and a shoulder to lean on. Instead, all you may experience is nothing but a myriad of rainy days, yet if you can stick around to the end of the storm for that moment when the sun peeks through and the most spectacular array of color sits hanging in the sky, you will see God's promise.

A Labor of Love

Jacob learned all too well about that break in the sky when he was blessed with the honor of having Rachel (the daughter of his uncle, Laban) as his wife. By the blessing and command of his father, Isaac, Jacob set out to Paddan Aram to find a wife among his mother's father, Bethuel. As Jacob arrived in town, there were several shepherds gathered near the well awaiting all the flocks to water the sheep. To Jacob's surprise, Rachel appeared with her flock. When he met her, the Bible (Genesis 29) says that Jacob immediately rolled the large stone away from the mouth of the well and watered his uncle's sheep. It was evident that Rachel was beyond gorgeous and had a glowing presence that made a man stand at attention. Jacob didn't ask any of the other shepherds to roll away the stone, nor did he half-serve by rolling the stone away and then letting Rachel water the sheep. No, he went all in! It was clear he was in love.

Jacob labored in love for an entire month for nothing. Then Laban offered to pay Jacob wages for his labor. Jacob responded with a proposal to work for Laban for seven years for Rachel's hand in marriage. After Jacob completed the seven years, he was told by his uncle that he had to work another seven years for Rachel, as she was the youngest daughter, and it was not custom to allow the youngest to marry first. Jacob gladly agreed to another seven years, as the last seven had felt like days to him. After those first seven years, not only did he receive Rachel as his wife, but he was also finally able to make love to her. Even after the marriage, Jacob kept his word and labored another seven years for her love as her husband. Jacob persevered fourteen years in total for Rachel's love.

A Timeless Love

God never promised it was always going to be easy. In fact, He said to follow Him there was a cost. It may get real rough, but make the decision to stay when it's the hardest to do so. True love doesn't give up or give in. It's in it for the long haul. It doesn't strategize or play fair-weather with its love. As you're crying out, "It's too hard," there could be a calm sea just on the other side but you refuse to accept the challenge. Love doesn't run in the opposite direction in the face of adversity. In fact, tough times don't change real love at all; it just goes in deeper and stronger. Our founding pastor of Concord Church, Dr. E. K. Bailey, would say that the difference between those who make it versus those who don't is commitment. The most beautiful kind of love is one that will stay in the game when it looks like all hope is lost. When your mate is in his or her darkest hour, love will patiently see them through. Your mate may be dealing with the loss of a child, deep depression, or just in a hopeless state. Are you going to peace out because everything isn't rosy, or are you going to get in the trenches and endure the valley? Anyone can relax and bask in the sunshine with you, but when it gets dark and ugly and the breeze turns into tornadoes, it takes real love to stay. His word says that when there are two, you have a better return but if one has to stand by himself, pity him (Ecclesiastes 4:9–10). Don't let your man or woman ride the tide alone. Be there in the turbulence; it will make for a deeper, richer relationship.

My grandmother was living and teaching in a small town in northern Mississippi when she met my grandfather. He owned a neighborhood store (attached to his home) about thirty minutes down the road from where my grandmother lived. They were introduced by my grandmother's coworker, who lived nearby. But grandmother said she didn't know about my grandfather (her chuckling). My grandfather was a jokester and sociable in nature, as was to be expected of a businessman in a small town, while grandmother was more of a reserved spirit.

My grandparents would get to know one another through conversation and later through courtship. They never "got together," as my grandmother would put it. Then, one day, my grandfather asked my grandmother to marry him, and she said, "Yes!" They would remain married for forty-nine years until my grandfather lost his bout with cancer in the summer of 2012.

During their marriage, my grandmother and I would have conversations on occasion about relationships. The best advice that she gave me was to never discuss your private matters with those outside of your marriage. She indicated that not only does it dishonor your spouse, but it brings drama to the relationship by involving others in your marital challenges. She says you are to go to your spouse directly about any grievances you have with him.

When I asked my grandmother what the reason for the success of their marriage was, she said that she prayed for him and for herself, and that through the prayers and the help of the Lord, they learned to hold on to each other. She said you must never give up on one another. My grandparents had their ups and downs, but my grandmother would say that the ups were more often than the downs. She said even when they had different likes, they still supported one another's decisions. She didn't always like or agree with everything my grandfather did, but she accepted his choices, and eventually things worked themselves out. She says she still thinks about my grandfather and will remain committed to him until God calls her home to be reunited with him again.

Love in Action: Perseverance

1. Pray that God will teach you how to stay and learn to love the one He's entrusting to you forever. Pray for discernment for relationships that are meant for a purpose, a season versus a lifetime.

2. When you're tempted to give up, remind yourself of the cost of starting over.

3. Make a commitment to love someone beyond the emotional stuff. Learn to respect and support their individual choices. Learn how to hold on to each other during the raging storms. Don't give up.

LEARNING TO LOVE

CHAPTER 16:
LOVING GOD

*Love the Lord your God with all your heart and with all your soul
and with all your mind and with all your strength. -Mark 12:30*

HOW CAN YOU NOT LOVE HIM? WHAT IS THERE NOT to love about God, the One who created every single good and perfect detail about you? You love Him because He first loved you (1 John 4:19). He had you in mind before you were ever conceived. He knew you even before your own mother knew you. He gave you breath. He gave you life. Nothing about you is a mistake. In His creation of you alone, God expressed His very love for you. And if that wasn't enough, He took drastic measures to establish a direct connection with you by coming down to earth in the form of Himself as His son. In His unconditional love for you, He gave His only son and divine creation of Himself over to death so that every single sin you will ever commit against Him would be forgiven. Through that unfailing commitment of love for you, you get another chance at life every single day with new grace and new mercies.

God shows up in your everyday just to let you know He's always near. "No one has ever seen God; but if we love one another, God lives in us and His love is made complete in us" (1 John 4:12). He is the myriad angels you encounter on a daily basis: the one who called just to see how you were doing, the one who held the door for you, and the one who delayed your departure to prevent you from that accident ahead. Whatever you need, He will provide. He affirms, "And I will do whatever you ask in my name, so that the Son may bring glory to the Father" (John 14:13). He sent His son to die for your salvation. He allows the Holy Spirit to intervene on your behalf when you have nothing to say or give. The Holy Spirit will stand in the gap for you and pray for you when words simply won't come out. He speaks through His creation so that you may hear His voice and know His way. If you need help, He will send a helper. If you need uplifting, He will send an encourager. And if love is all you need, just look to Him.

You know Him because He created the world. Creation is He. When you're walking along the beach and the ocean comes to shore and stops at a certain point, you have to know that has God written all over it, not science or evolution. That first cry from a baby at birth, how could man know to do that? The backdrop of the sky alone is evidence of His glory.

In any relationship, to know someone, you must spend time with them. You study their habits, what makes them smile, and what breaks their heart. If you love them, you want to do things for them that make them smile. You avoid those things that break their hearts. Loving God requires much of the same. You must spend time with Him getting to know Him. Those things you innately want to be and/or do are the things that make Him smile. Those things that break His heart break yours too.

Getting to know God requires spending time in His word and studying His habits. The more you get to know Him and honor His commandments, the greater the depth of your relationship with Him. Moreover, when you treat others with love, love for God is expressed in your obedience to His law. He knew we wouldn't be perfect as the world sees perfect, but through His love, He knew we would be made flawless.

We could spend a lifetime trying to analyze God and calculate His moves. We could say, "Because He blessed Mary in that manner, He can do the same for me." If you've known God for some time, you know that He simply can't be put in a box like that. When "bad" things happen, we may want to believe that God doesn't love us or that we did something wrong, but that is not how God loves. Please, please know that He doesn't do things to hurt you. He will, however, allow an event in your life to occur to define you or refine you. If you are a parent, you know your child. You know that there will be things that you will simply have to tell your child no to because it is not in his or her best interest. Sometimes the answer is, "Not now." And when he or she is ready, the "not now" becomes a strong "YES." As such, when God withholds something from you, it is because "that thing" was not in your best interest. But when you're ready, He will send a "new thing," and it will be beyond what you could have ever hoped for or conceived of in your mind.

Trusting God may not make sense to the human mind. He says to remember the Sabbath and keep it holy. He requires us to rest at least one day a week and enjoy the fruits of our labor. He wants you to trust in your rest that He is still able to do His best work and handle the details in your absence. When my schedule gets hectic and I am running all week and have deadlines to meet, it's tempting to want to skip church and use that time to do "my work." But the love relationship I have with God won't let me skip on those Sundays when I'm trying to buy more time. If I were to calculate the number of hours and all I have slated to do, to steal away time just to worship Him just doesn't make sense. But because of all He has done for me, I want to honor Him with a body of believers in His house. Church for me is not a religious tradition or weekly ritual, it's desiring to spend time in fellowship with my Father. So I go, and the blessing I receive through His word as well as the connection with other men and women of faith far outweighs my need to work. Although the hours to worship and rest don't add up, somehow God always works out the details in our lives when we give it over to Him.

His love language is quality time, so when I give Him that, He gives me more of Him in abundant ways. So love Him by trusting Him with it all.

The Church

I grew up catching the bus to church or attending with my parents. At a very young age, I came to know the gift of salvation and accepted Christ as my personal Savior. As part of the Christian community and body of believers, I am bothered with how we treat others at times. We can be so passionate about the mission but also so wrong. Our approach with the right attitude can make a world of difference in the life of a nonbeliever or a new follower. As believers, we can operate in a Pharisee mentality and focus on stuff that has nothing to do with anything. From chewing gum in church to a woman wearing a pair of slacks, we can major on the minor when the real aim is to save souls.

For me, the church has served as a source of accountability for making good decisions that are aligned with God's will versus my own plans. The way you live your life is the most credible window people get to see a God they may have never known. As Christians, we have to be really careful about how we demonstrate God's love toward others. We forget sometimes that we were once nonbelievers and needed that unconditional, no-strings-attached kind of love to draw us to the One who can change everything. We can get very self-righteous and instead of displaying love, we can make a mockery of Christianity through our condescension, disrespect, and hypocrisy. We can make Christianity look like anything but love. We must remember that Christianity is not about what we don't do (i.e., I don't cheat on my wife; I don't rob God of His tithe; I don't go to clubs). Nevertheless, what we do is what can lead others astray: I do kill with looks of disdain when you order a glass of wine; I do watch and wait for your every mishap and make sure I sound the trumpets when you do; I do rob you of encouragement when I withhold from telling you how great of a job you did. He encourages us not to be a stumbling block for others (1 Corinthians 8:9–11), so be an ambassador of love and compassion; it's a much richer reward, and you're much more attractive when you adorn yourself with humility and exude peace.

The church is full of hypocrites, you might be saying. I get it. Indeed, God set the standard for how we are to love and treat one another yet someone failed you. I love God, and I love the church. Nonetheless, I understand that loving God is not a membership into a religious institution. It's a personal relationship with an all-knowing and all-loving God. He knows how to handle those who are disobedient to His standard of love, yet His love is available to all... even the hypocrites. Don't let those who haven't learned how to truly love God keep you from fully experiencing the most important relationship you'll ever have and know. "It is not the healthy who need a doctor, but the sick. But go and learn what this means: 'I desire mercy, not sacrifice.' For I have not come to call the righteous, but sinners" (Matthew 9:12–13).

The Pharisees were extremely religiously focused and lived by the letter of the law of God's word. They believed in the burial and resurrection and even eternal life. Yet, they forgot about the people. They were so focused on the law that they neglected the one ingredient God required most: love. They were caught up in the rules of the law and forcing that same law down the throats of others when they themselves often fell short. Their judgment of others was not only hypocritical, but it was a false sense of love for God's people that hurt relationships and a desired relationship with the Father. They enjoyed the prestige of being considered one of piety. Ironically, a people who believed in the resurrection clearly missed the reason for Christ's cause. Christ came to save us, but they acted as if salvation depended upon their good and how well they could live up to the law. The Sadducees, on the other hand, were politically minded. They often questioned The Book. They were the ones who were not feeling the church and were always asking, "Is it Old Testament or New Testament?" If it was Old Testament doctrine, they were challenging the practices and would argue with you that it wasn't God's word. How they concluded what was possible was through their own intellect. Belief in God was shaky while status and influence were their greatest cause. They would sell their souls for a ranked seat.

When I meet people who share with me that they are not a religious person but they believe in God and/or communicate with Him daily, I get super excited. I think the fact that they aren't a religious person is a great thing, as the mission is a personal relationship. Religion was meant to provide a structure or road map of guidelines for living God's way. But there are some who have taken those guidelines out of context to serve their own agendas while others simply haven't been taught better or even know better. In an attempt to serve God, they have good intentions, yet their intentions get poorly served because they haven't learned the difference between judgment and accountability. For me, that is why the church exists.

The church is the place of assembly for preparation for the big game. The work you do within the church is practice time. The pastor is the head coach while the associate ministers serve as the defensive and offensive coordinators. The body of believers is likened to a team of players, all with different skills and abilities who uniquely contribute to the game of life. The object of the game is to win souls for Christ. Yet the strategy is to love others unconditionally just as Christ loves us. The playbook is the Bible. It gives you all the instructions you will ever need to win the game. Yet, as a player on the team, sometimes you can interpret the instructions beautifully while other times you may need some guidance. And that's a great thing. However, when you choose to go out on the playing field alone without any coaching, you risk personal foul and injury. The key to winning is making sure you're on a good team and have a good coach. But you can't spend all your days on the practice field. You have to play in the game. The game is played beyond the walls of the church. Where we can fail as Christians is getting stuck in the assembly. Gather to get the instructions, and then get back in the game. The gathering only serves as a checkpoint or place of accountability to know what you can tighten up to get a win. Those teammates who are failing in their plays (rendering judgment on others, abusing the playbook, or using the game to give glory to themselves) need your love and accountability just as much as the world does. Instead of seeing them as the opponent, recognize we're all on the same team. You have to be obedient to the strategy to win. Just about every story that was ever told in the Bible was tied to winning in life as a result of having a loving, personal relationship with the Father. It's all for His glory.

A Personal Relationship

I met Nicole in Fort Myers, Florida, during the summer preceding my senior year in college. We were both interns for GE's Financial Management Program, she from Tuskegee and I from Langston. Nicole was very sharp and always on top of her game. I loved her strong, passionate spirit, and her laugh was simply infectious. She would be my roomie for the summer. The gentleman I was dating at the time would swing by our apartment on Sunday mornings to pick me up for church. We would invite Nicole on several occasions to attend with us, but she would respectfully decline each time. When we asked why, she mentioned that she hadn't had good experiences with church, so we tried not to force the invitations.

After that summer, Nicole and I lost contact for a few years. Then, one day when I was in the professional workforce, I received a call from her. When we spoke, the majority of her conversation was about God. She spoke about her commitment to God as well as her relationship with God. I kept thinking, "Wow, is this my same roommate from Fort Myers who kept declining the invites to attend church?" Her heart and passion for God were so refreshing! I had been in the church since I was a little girl, but this beautiful woman of God was on fire for Him, more on fire than I had been all my years. I asked her during our call what changed. She shared with me that it was through a book that she had been reading that she finally got it. The book was about a man who was struggling with a same-sex attraction and went to the church for help. When the man met with the pastor, the pastor completely took advantage of the vulnerability of this man. At that experience, the man made a decision to stop going to church. Later, the man would start going to church again only this time to learn that church was less about the measure of others and more about his personal relationship with God. It was this revelation that helped Nicole understand that going to church was about a personal relationship with God.

During her childhood, church wasn't something they did together as a family on a regular basis. They would attend church on Easter, but it wasn't a practice in their household. When Nicole was a freshman in high school, she would attend with a friend of hers. Her friend was in the choir, so it seemed logical to Nicole to also join the choir. Nicole, however, had a sports injury and had to wear a brace on her leg. Because of her brace, she showed up to church with pants on. She was informed at that time that she couldn't wear pants in the choir stand. Nicole explained why she was wearing the pants, and the lady said she understood but again informed Nicole that she could not wear pants at the church. Since Nicole was really joining the choir to hang out with her friend, she lost all interest to come back.

Years would pass, and Nicole would attend church again during her freshman year in college from time to time with friends on their home visit from college. During a particular visit, the church would ask everyone to contribute two hundred dollars in addition to their regular tithe and offering. Nicole asked, "What if I don't have two hundred dollars? Will they take a hundred dollars?" She thought it was interesting that the pastor would be very nicely suited while the congregation didn't represent that same level of dress. She had questions about why there was a building fund but no building plans in view. That personal relationship with God was something that just wasn't modeled for her, nor did anyone guide her through that process or answer any of her questions.

Later, Nicole, a business major, would meet Terrence, an engineering major, at Tuskegee. Nicole had plenty of classes in the engineering building, but they had never met until Terrence was just a few months away from graduating. The moment Terrence met Nicole, he said he knew she would be his wife. But because they shared different lifestyles at that stage, Terrence had some questions about God's choice for him. Terrence was very grounded spiritually and was not big on alcoholic drink or going to clubs. Nicole, on the other hand, knew God but didn't frequent the church and would occasionally have a drink; she was always the designated driver, but she enjoyed a good party here and there. Unbeknownst to Nicole, God was priming her for Terrence.

After Terrence graduated, he and Nicole kept in touch, developed a beautiful friendship, and later dated. During this time, Nicole was befriended by a Christian lady at work. Nicole began visiting church with her and her husband. They became Nicole's spiritual parents. They would guide her through her questions about God, the church, and the Bible. In addition, Nicole and Terrence would have Bible study over the phone every other week as well as watch a TV evangelist who provided them both with in-depth biblical teaching. Her spiritual growth from there became a natural progression.

Nicole lived in two other cities after college graduation and always found a church where she would worship, but she was noncommittal in terms of joining a congregation and wanted to make sure the church was nondenominational. She never felt 100 percent at home and still had questions about how to live the lifestyle of a Christian. Nicole would eventually return to her hometown in Southern California. By God's design, Terrence ended up there, too.

In prior relationships, Nicole would give 70 percent while asking her guy to give 100 percent. She realized as she began to mature that it should always be 100 percent and was devoted to giving that in her next committed relationship, which would be with Terrence. The two made a commitment to join a church and be active. Nicole would learn from Terrence about growing as an individual; he helped her to heal from past hurts from her childhood relationships. Terrence would learn from Nicole that, as Christians, we can be hypocritical and miss the mark.

Nicole and Terrence were married in 2002 after a seven-year, organically grown friendship turned courtship. They thought they were waiting to pursue their individual career goals, but in retrospect, they realized professional priorities shouldn't be a reason to delay matrimony and learned that they were greater together than apart. The good thing about their years of completion was that it allowed them to build a solid foundation and truly get to know one another. They knew without a doubt what they were signing up for, so they had no surprises later in the marriage. They founded their relationship and marriage on 1 Corinthians 13. God was prepping Nicole for Terrence all along; however, Terrence would have missed her if he hadn't recognized that she was in seed form when he met her. It was through his watering her with love and the showering of prayers, not only from him but from her mother and grandparents too, that Nicole would become this woman who is sold out for God.

Because of that experience, she encourages others not to overlook a potential spouse because they are in seed form. Every time I talk to Nicole, I leave our conversations or visits renewed. She has such a love for God and takes the time to explain her love to others so that there is no confusion, should you have questions. Who knew back in that summer in Fort Myers how instrumental she would be in my own life. Anytime she comes into contact with knowledge, be it spiritually, personally, or professionally, she will pick up the phone or send me an e-mail to say, "Hey, thought this may be of interest to you." Her integrity is even more refreshing. It's clear she does it because she loves Him.

Nicole says it is through her relationship with God that her marriage is easy work. She says it's hard to be selfish when you allow the Holy Spirit to self-correct. She says she is mindful of what she says to Terrence, as she knows whatever she puts out can't be taken back. Nicole says their marriage is a process of forever sowing seed and reaping the harvest. They just celebrated thirteen years of marriage and twenty years of togetherness. Now, that's how you witness for God!

Love in Action: Loving God

1. If you don't have a personal relationship with God and would like to know Him, invite Him into your life. Romans 10:9–10 provides guidance on how to ask Him to be your Lord and Savior. Pray: "Dear God, I would like a personal relationship with you and would like you to be Lord of my life. I have sinned, yet I believe your son, Jesus, died on the cross and was raised to life to save me from my sins. I receive you as my personal Lord and Savior. In Jesus's name, amen."

2. Spend at least ten minutes of uninterrupted private time each day getting to know God better through prayer, studying His word, and/or worshipping His name through song or speech.

3. Take some time to introduce yourself to a total stranger. Ask if he or she has a personal relationship with God. Share the gospel (without judgment) with your newfound friend.

CHAPTER 17:
LOVING SELF

After all, no one ever hated his own body, but he feeds and cares for it, just as Christ does the church. -Ephesians 5:29

I HAD HEARD PEOPLE TALK ABOUT LOVING YOURSELF; but for a long time, I didn't truly understand what it meant until I stopped putting so much pressure on myself and started giving myself the freedom to choose my own path, undefined by anyone else. I learned that love is knowing that I don't have to do it all, but that God can. Not only did I not have to do it all, I learned that I didn't always have to *do* and could allow myself to just *be*. I learned to allow my heart to mend, to accept His mercy and grace for my past, and to look toward my future with expectancy for even better tomorrows. I learned to take in the joy, the laughter, and to accept His gift.

Yet, we're so busy with being busy that we often neglect what's most important. We miss the beauty in our day. We miss the small whispers because there is so much noise that it's hard to hear any kind of leading or direction. We miss the birds chirping. The scales may not always balance, but at least shoot for some equilibrium in your life. You need to allow yourself love.

Your Thoughts are Love

You are what you believe you are. Whatever you think is what you exude in your life. If you don't like yourself, how do you expect others to? If you are always thinking negatively or jumping to conclusions, you will attract negativity and defeat. Do you find yourself concocting thoughts in your head about a situation, only to find out you were overanalyzing and it was all in your head? Don't put your thoughts on other people. If you think thoughts of positivity, the sky is not even the limit for where you can and will end up.

The height of the potential of a person can be easily determined by the conversation of their lips. Speak edification to your hopes and dreams. Love yourself enough to change your thoughts; change your stinking thinking. Love does not pity itself. When someone asks you how you are doing or how your day was, how do you respond? Are you grateful for another day, or do you focus on all that went wrong? Learn to operate in the love zone and expect the best always. When the horizon has always looked bleak, maybe it shouldn't be you waiting on change in your life but maybe that change should be in you. Maybe, just maybe, life is waiting on you. When you're ready, you will see your landscape change. The desolate wasteland suddenly becomes a rich oasis, and the view is breathtaking—nothing like anything you've ever seen before—all because you finally chose to love yourself or love yourself better.

Have Faith

You must believe He wants you to experience a great life. Your plans may not have manifested themselves, but please know that is truly okay. Know that the death of your plans could very well be the best thing that ever happened to you. Relinquish the control. Be open to the outcome. Anxiety and urgency is nothing but fear. Fear is only as strong as you created it to be. Just as faith as a mustard seed can move mountains, fear the size of a poppy seed can kill your dreams.

Get uncomfortable and learn to take a risk. Not long ago, a wise man shared a story with me about the eagle stirring her nest. He explained that the bottom of the nest is made up of sharp thorny branches, which is covered by lots of cushioning for the baby eagles. When the mother is ready for the baby eagles to fly, she will stir her nest, causing the thorny portion to be exposed and incite her babies to fly. If they won't fly on their own, then she will drop them from the nest. And if that still doesn't work, the babies will drop to their death. "Without faith, it's impossible to please Him" (Hebrew 11:6).

Know Your Worth

It is of the utmost importance that you know and understand your worth. If not, you will define your existence and purpose based on the external rather than the internal. Accordingly, when you allow others to be the author of love in your life, the "love" (good or bad) they impart to you becomes the "love" you come to know. Instead of waiting for others to define "love" for you, you must come to know it for yourself. You must choose what is important to you and make sure that you gift yourself with the best every single day of your life.

It's true that it takes time to get to know people and determine whether he or she is someone you will allow to sit at your table. In every relationship, there is the process of getting to know someone. However, I get discouraged when I see my sisters allowing men to string them along and never present them as the queens they are. She says he's her "friend," never "boyfriend." It hurts my heart when I see a good woman lower her standards, never to win a prize but just so a man will show her some attention. Live life, but don't do it desperately. When you're thirsty, it shows, especially to him. When he sees your thirstiness, he knows you don't value yourself. Men don't value thirsty; the wrong ones take advantage of it, using it to their advantage.

I hate to see a good man being disrespected or controlled by his lady. You can see it in his body language that he isn't happy, yet she doesn't seem to notice it at all. At the end of the day, you are the common denominator in every one of your relationships. People can only do what you enable so stop being an enabler of bad behavior. That doesn't mean you eighty-six the relationship; it just means you kill the need to be esteemed in an unhealthy way. Make a positive change about the way you think about yourself. Teach others how to love you by the love you show to yourself.

Be Honest

It can be uber tempting to live dishonestly but choose not to lie. Instead, choose the truth. When we lie, we say, "I'm not good enough just the way I am, so I must fabricate a reality that allows me to be loved in your eyes." I have flaws; we all have flaws. One of the best gifts I received from a friend was the ability to be my authentic self. He could see the hurt of my past and assured me he wasn't in my life to hurt me. He built such a sturdy bridge between us that it felt safe to walk on and connect with him on that bridge. He challenged me to allow him to see my flaws. Each time I did, he made two steps (to my one) toward a deeper bond. Before I could look up, he was standing before me to help me cross that bridge. When we arrived there safely, he said, "Your flaws are beautiful. I love your flaws, and you should show the world more often." He never used them against me, even later in our friendship. He made it a point to keep the bridge secure. We have to do better about being bridges for people. Two simple steps forward at a time could change someone's whole trajectory for a lifetime. We were put here to be a gift, so gift someone with the ability to be and grow.

Be honest about who you are. Lying says, "I don't trust you; I don't feel worthy of you the way I am." One of the biggest complaints in relationships is: "He or she is not who I met X years ago." Or, "He or she is not who I married." Ooooh, please don't buy into it. People will usually tell you who they are, but because we go into relationships emotionally, we exit emotionally when our emotional needs aren't met, creating this constant hamster wheel of damage and baggage. So we hide. You can be very good at hiding. Although very deceptive, I get why people hide. Life is defined by the culture we live in, so if who you are doesn't fit into the culture, then acceptance becomes an inhibitor in your relationship. You want to be loved, so you forfeit self-love for acceptance, but what they really see is a mirage of who you are. Stop hiding. Stop clinging to the deceit. It's not fair to the other person, nor is it fair to yourself. One day, the real you will have to take a break from that acting job of yours and when you do, I just pray the person in your life truly loves you enough to love you through it. I pray they are able to walk with you to help you remove the draperies you've been hiding behind. Choose to accept yourself. Have the courage to live it out in truth.

Embrace Your Uniqueness

Be you, and be your best you. Nobody can do you better than you can. You were fearfully and wonderfully made. What a gift from the Creator! I love that He made us all unique and with such authenticity. When you choose to mimic someone else's life, that's pure laziness. God wants you to unleash your creativity. God didn't make you to be a replica. If He had, He would have made everyone the same way. Even as identical twins, there is still that something…that mark that sets each one apart from the other. So if He is brilliant enough to establish you in His likeness yet in your uniqueness in the physical, don't you think He wants you to live your life by celebrating your authenticity and wholeness. And you can't live life whole by always doing it half.

Make Wise Choices

Love listens. We are all given a moral compass, that inner voice that tells us right from wrong and good from bad. The decision to listen to that voice determines your success. Whatever you choose is typically what will follow you. The road less traveled can be surprisingly wonderful but often not taken because of the fear of the unknown. The blessing about taking the path rooted in the law is that through God's instruction, you give yourself this most amazing life. Even with the twists and turns, you can rest knowing that goodness and mercy will soon follow. The misconception about taking the path of least resistance is that it can appear easy and fun and resemble the blessing, but that's just it, the enemy is cunning. Take the time to know His truth, not by what the world has defined as true. Invest in the livelihood of your future by making wise choices.

Learn to Say No

When you learn to say no to all that isn't good for you, the floodgates for all that is good begin to overflow in abundance! Loving yourself is not selfish. It's self-preservation. Loving yourself says I make myself a priority so that I have more to give to the world. If you don't learn to take care of yourself, life will make that decision for you. One of my biggest character flaws has been my inability to say no. I am the queen of "Yes." I simply love helping others. I love seeing people reach their fullest potential. I've been someone who wants to see everyone happy and at peace, so I have said yes a lot of times to accomplish just that. The thing about saying yes to most everything is that it leaves little room for yourself. God said we are to work six days and rest on the Sabbath. He knew we needed rest. In fact, He highly recommends it. By doing so, you demonstrate an intimate level of trust in Him to do His part, while you simply rest. Without it, you begin to operate on autopilot, on fumes, and out of exhaustion. That's not a good place to be. Allowing yourself to rest just doesn't logically add up, especially when you have a million and one things to take care of and there are only so many hours in a day. Yet, if you just learn to give yourself a break without guilt, your giving to others will come from a full tank and greater energy. You will actually have more to give when you save something for yourself. Then, your giving comes from a position of power.

Forgive Yourself

Don't look back! It's injurious to keep rehearsing the hurt. Forfeit the instant replays. Otherwise you will get stuck in the paralysis of analysis. Keep your eyes on the road ahead. Know and trust that there was a reason (even if not understood) for whatever didn't happen.

Don't judge yourself. Who hasn't fallen hard? Everyone has said or done something they are not proud of. The worst thing you can do is dwell on it. You stifle any forward movement and cripple yourself from enjoying the precious moment that is right in front of you. Suffering is a choice. Stop the self-inflicting wounds. Forgiveness allows you to free yourself from the bondage of your former choices. It allows you to love yourself.

Do you remember that moment when someone extended grace and forgiveness toward you? Remember how it felt like someone had just removed a ton of bricks from your shoulders? Take a moment to live in that moment and just bask in that forgiveness. When you forgive yourself, you give yourself that same kind of unpacking of bags from an extended trip of pain, grief, and suffering. You make the decision to move from that old address of guilt and shame and tell the self-defeating voices, "Fear doesn't live here anymore. Love lives here." You have to get up from that self-loathing stupor of yours and be intently present. You have a life to live, so live it!

Rock It Out

As we know it, we only get one life here on earth, so rock it out and enjoy it to the utmost! See the world. Experience all kinds of cultures; it will allow to you to see the globe from different perspectives and with an empathetic heart. Laugh often and laugh loudly. Make sure you are getting what you need every single day of your life; you will have more to offer when you do. Learn something new every day. Share your knowledge and joys with others. Give the gift of being your absolute best to all of God's creation. Make time to connect face-to-face and one-on-one. Smile from the inside and allow it to radiate your external self. Relax. Relax. Relax. Be still, listen, and enjoy the sound of your breathing. You have life. Don't abuse the gift. Don't give anyone the power to alter your best efforts. If you're going to build something, build bridges, families, and homes. Love. Love. Love some more…

Love in Action: Loving Self

1. Petition God to teach you how to love yourself in a selfless and healthy way. Ask Him to reveal to you areas in which you need to learn to give yourself some grace.

2. Create a self-love list of things you would like to see manifested in your life. Make sure you get at least one of those things daily.

3. Identify something you've always wanted to do but just seemed to never have the time or resources for. Make a plan to see it into fruition in the next ninety days.

CHAPTER 18:
LOVING THROUGH
COURTSHIP

He who finds a wife finds what is good and receives
favor from the Lord. -Proverbs 18:22

WHEN A MAN IS READY FOR COMMITMENT, HE WILL make it very clear. You won't have to wonder what you are doing or what your status is. He won't give you vague terms like "we're just kicking it" or "just getting to know one another." He won't string you along or play games with you. There are not enough miles between you that can keep him from getting to you. The excuses will be nonexistent. The world will know you are his because he won't be able to keep it to himself.

When a woman is ready for commitment, she will give you her whole heart, so be sure to take great care of it. She will give you a place of leadership and priority in her life. She won't string you along or play games with you. There are not enough words that can express her appreciation for you. The excuses will be nil. She will stand by your side and support you as the head of your future family. The world will know you are hers because she won't be able to keep it to herself.

Dating vs. Courting

Courtship was instituted as a serious commitment between a couple to prepare for engagement and marriage. Dating was later introduced in the late 1800s and early 1900s and has gradually removed the layer of protection for a woman that courtship provided. As the years have passed, dating has taken precedence, and each generation has redefined dating to serve its own time. Courtship, although it still exists, is almost a distant term in today's age.

There are so many different meanings of dating that it's important that you know before going in what it means to you as well as the person you're entertaining. Dating says, "I'm interested and would like to try you on." Courting says, "I know what I want and am ready to make a commitment for a lifetime." The thing about most dating is that it gives you a false sense of relationship. It likes all the benefits of having a relationship but without all of the responsibility. Often times when dating sees commitment in view, it will run for the hills. Courtship says, "I am not here to play games and am not going to string you along. You are not simply someone I'm dating; I'm making plans, God willing, to make you my wife."

Dating also creates an illusion of love that is driven by lust. Sex is free to explore because we are all adults, right? Even as adults, we can still make childlike decisions that are focused on a selfish want to satisfy the flesh. Courtship honors the biblical context of sex to be served only in the marital covenant. Nevertheless, when the world says dating is the standard for relationships and few will take a stand for greater, then it's really tough to stand alone in that pursuit to be a facilitator for change. In the end, someone always gets hurt when we choose to do it our way versus what He told us to do in the first place.

Be Who You Want to Attract

Be who and what you want to attract. If you want someone who is family oriented, figure out what family oriented really means to you and be that. If you want someone who is committed, be a person of promise. If you want to have kids, learn what a child needs. I don't think relationships magically establish those things. I've heard people say, "When I get married, it will be different; I'll be this type of person when I get married," but when they get married, they struggle with that same aspect of their character they were before the marriage. They played the field for so long that they never practiced the position they said they wanted to have. They unconsciously trained themselves to be this other person that by the time they got married, they didn't know how to be anyone other than the person they had always been. I believe you have to become what you want even prior to the relationships. I think relationships can help you grow if you allow them, but they don't establish you. Who you are is who you are; however, you can choose to be more, but you have to be willing to put in the work to get to that person. To be realized, your behaviors and values must align.

Could This Be Love?

Love is not attraction; attraction is not love, as attraction can fade with time. Infatuation is not love, nor is being in love with the idea of love. An idea is not the person in front of you, flaws and all. Sometimes it can be all "emotional," and we're trying to convince ourselves it's from God. Love is not a fantasy built on emotions or a series of emotional highs. Romance does not equal love. Although flattering, don't mistake someone's kindness to mean love; love alone is not a string of nice gestures (grandiose or slight). It is not always a feel good sensation or about making another person happy. Love is not a search-and-rescue mission. It's not something you beg for. Love is not just something you speak. Simply a word, love is not.

Love is more than a feeling. Love equals commitment. The feeling of love and the commitment of love must go hand in hand. Love is organically inclined to present itself and is always attracted to love. It's a choice, a promise to love forever through the good, the bad, and the ugly. Anything other than that is an imitation.

Getting to Know

Knowledge is power. Most studies have indicated that it only takes about four minutes to determine if you like someone; but it takes a lifetime to get to know them. Take time to get to know the person in front of you. Find out what's most important to him or her. Luke 12:34 points out, "For where your treasure is, there your heart will be also." What occupies the priority of his or her heart? What do they like to do for fun? What makes her smile? What makes him laugh? Understand what fills their tank.

A closed mouth doesn't get fed. As you gather information about the person in front of you, know that there is a fine line between taking time to get to know someone and wasting the other person's time. It really doesn't take a long time for you to decide if you want to be with someone. You either want the relationship or you don't. It's really that simple. I think we make relationships more complicated than they need to be because of our own selfish agendas.

Consistent nonexclusive dating with the same people is just an excuse for a person to explore other relationships while having the freedom to have you on standby should they decide to entertain your company. Sadly, we accept the crumbs on both sides (male and female) that are being served and the lie that we're just getting to know one another. Please don't get me wrong; I'm not saying not to take the time to ask the questions and observe the character to see if the person is a good match for you. By all means, please do so. But when the consideration to move forward with anything tangible is constantly prefaced with "we're just getting to know each other," he or she has likely placed you in the "in the meantime" bucket. Keep in mind that you will always be getting to know one another even after marriage.

If you know the person in front of you is looking for commitment and you're only looking for fun, be selfless and be gone. Don't be selfish and hold up a spot that someone more worthwhile would appreciate. If you're looking for commitment and the other person is looking for fun, it's just as much your responsibility to say no when you know you want so much more. Share your convictions and hopes up front; don't shy away or be timid. A person knows what they want when they want it, so don't let them waste your time prolonging what you already know to be true…you're not "wifey," or you're not "hubby." You delay your ability to make a good choice by dancing around what it is you truly desire out of a relationship. You teach the other person what you're willing to accept by what you respond to. Guard the wellspring of your heart. Value your time.

True love awakens vulnerability. Establish open and honest communication that permits a loving trust. Be fearless in your sharing and patient in your listening. The person won't ever know what you don't share. You won't ever know what the person will do with what you share, if you don't. The choice to establish a deep-loving connection is yours for the making.

Know your connecting style. If you're someone who needs phone and/or face-to-face interaction, be true to that as you're planning to be in this for the long-haul. Someone who enjoys texting as a primary means of communication and interaction may not be a good match. Make sure your connecting is not just a habit of routine but that you're truly reaching the other person where it matters most.

Get to know the family and friends. You will learn a lot about your potential mate from those with whom they spend the most of their time. Whom they spend their time with will be whom you spend your time with too. You don't just marry him or her, you marry the total package. It's not always a tell-all, but it does serve as a great guide.

Embrace the disagreements. You will learn more about the person in a disagreement than in all the nice and easy stuff. There will be things that will just require discussion to go deeper in your relationship. How well you are able to resolve conflict will speak volumes about your future as one. Be more of a lover than a fighter, but don't be afraid to know depth.

At the end of the day, get to know but don't overanalyze. Love is not a checklist or a long list of criteria. Have standards but don't get so bogged down in things that don't serve anything. Remember to enjoy the process; good relationships don't get realized or birthed in tension. Whether things work out with this person or not, do your best to leave the person better and not bitter.

Making a Wise Choice

Marriage is serious. Choosing who you will spend the rest of your life with is one of the most important decisions you will ever make, if not the most important decision. Your picking will be vital to your long-term health. Make a wise decision. I truly believe marriage is easy to get into but hard to get out of. The breaking of a covenant that God intended to be for a lifetime can leave lots of tears and scars. What are you seeking to build your marriage on?

Before you commit, consider the character. The character is the part of the soul that will choose to do the right thing even when it doesn't have an audience. Is it easy for her to lie? Is telling the truth always of the utmost importance to him? Does she honor her word, or can you never depend on her to do what she said she would do? It's highly probable that what you see is what you get. Can you be your best self with this person? Do they steal away pieces of your soul? Don't expect the person to be you; there is only one you. But consider someone who is already in a place where you're trying to go or at least on the same flight as you.

Foundationally, choose a mate who shares your morals and values. Do they at least have a heart for God? Do they fear Him? Does the person draw you closer to Christ, or do you find yourself drifting further from God as a result of your relationship with them? Second Corinthians 6:14 (KJV) states, "Be ye not unequally yoked together with unbelievers: for what fellowship hath righteousness with unrighteousness? And what communion hath light with darkness?" Don't expect the other person to be your savior. There is only one Savior. The key is that they help you be better in Christ and your spiritual life.

A key thing to always remember: it is the man that findeth a wife, not a woman that findeth a husband. When a woman tries to assume that role, it distorts the order and removes the woman from the covering and protection God intended for her. As a woman, you will rob yourself of a beautiful pursuit and courtship if you don't learn to trust God's choice for you. Welcome the pursuit!

Submit One to the Other

"Submit to one another out of reverence for Christ" (Ephesians 5:21). Submitting can sometimes, if not most times, be a challenge. It's letting go and trusting someone to have your back with the greatest good. When you have been doing it for so long by yourself, it can be quite uncomfortable and hard to allow someone else to be there for you. Get comfortable with the discomfort and learn to just be. Learn to receive help and trust the help. Learn to submit.

"Wives, submit to your husbands as to the Lord" (Ephesians 5:22). A good man desires and enjoys the responsibility of leading his family. Believe it or not, he likes the pressure of responsibility. He enjoys helping out and seeing his woman smile. Conversely, when a woman tries to take ownership of his leading, that journey becomes less gratifying. Allow him the position as the head of the family; follow his lead of God's lead. You permit him that when you pray for him, respect him, accept more of his suggestions than you give counter-offers, and encourage him to be the best man he desires to be for himself, you, and the family.

"Husbands, love your wives, just as Christ loved the church and gave Himself up for her" (Ephesians 5:25). A woman desires to be the helpmate. She may hold it down at work, but when she comes home, she most often does not want any responsibility of leading. However, when the man chooses passivity instead of being the covering, it can be tough not to try rising to the occasion. She needs to be cared for and nurtured as she does for others. She loves it when you have made plans with her likes in mind. Love her by praying regularly for her and allowing her the ability to just be feminine.

God's Design for Sex

Sex is to be motivated by love and commitment, not lust, and it should be protected by the covenant of marriage. However, sex is one set of instructions we try to edit in relationships yet feel the most destruction when not obeyed. Song of Songs 3:5 encourages, "Do not arouse or awaken love until it so desires."

One of the rewarding benefits of courtship is that it heartens a conviction to align one's sexual desires with God's intended design. Sex was fashioned as a wonderful gift to be shared between a husband and a wife, not a dating couple or boyfriend and girlfriend. As sex is one of the most natural of activities that God created, it can equally become the most nasty when we seek to explore it outside of His core design. The repercussions of being disobedient to His model are endless. From sexually transmitted diseases to unwanted pregnancies, the consequences can render great pain. He knew the harm it would cause outside of marriage, so He set boundaries in place for our ultimate protection.

Even knowing the consequences, we rationalize and make excuses as to why it's okay: "I have needs. It's a natural desire. Everyone else is doing it." In an age where so much about relationships has become casual (i.e., friends with benefits), if you don't guard your heart, the effects could be detrimental. We still have to be true to self while still being open to new possibilities or paths we may not have planned for but so much more rewarding. That's where prayer and godly discernment come into play.

Some will try to use the "closing of legs" to manipulate a proposal, but that is not what this journey was intended for. Your choosing to wait until marriage should be to honor you and God foremost. Love yourself enough to have standards and surround yourself with those who have been successful in those standards. God will indeed reward your faithfulness.

Time of Preparation for Marriage

Your courtship should be the time where you begin to prepare for a marital relationship. It is where you discuss the vision for your future and make tangible plans to see that vision to fruition. Those plans must first be covered by God's leading and His will. I strongly encourage you to seek wise premarital counseling as you prepare for your new life as one. It will help make you aware of your blind spots and provide you with preventive measures and tools to handle the bumps you will encounter along the road. Nothing is damage-proof, but prayerfully you will be more prepared should you encounter great difficulties. You wouldn't purchase a car without some kind of preventive maintenance plan or warranty in place. The more you are to focus on the preventive maintenance, the less likely you will have major costly repairs down the road. If you encounter issues, you have a covering for the ride that won't leave you penniless. You could purchase the car without any maintenance plan or warranty; but if you find out you have a lemon, the cost alone to fix your car could wreak havoc on your pocketbook, not to mention the mental stress of constantly having to manage the unexpected woes. If you aren't remotely prepared to deal with such a challenge, it could very well become increasingly tempting to leave that car abandoned. You might be saying, "I can always just go get a new car, right?" You could, as it's your choice, but at some point, it would be wise to have a plan in place for the long-haul. Why not start from the beginning to do the right thing? Don't make the costly mistake not to make the wise investment from day one. Care enough about your future to take the time and make the necessary plans for a lasting, loving marriage.

The Art of Courtship

Tara and Franklin met in July 2013 at a jazz concert in Addison Park. Tara had just moved to Dallas, Texas, three months prior, so she was still getting acclimated to the city. She would attend the jazz concert with her girlfriend that summer day. Heading into the park, Tara's girlfriend stopped to say hello to her friends, one of which was a coworker of Franklin's. Franklin was in the middle of a conversation with the couple at that time. Tara noticed Franklin, but he couldn't see that she was checking him out behind her shades. Because of her biblical teachings, she knew that it was a man that findeth, so she held back from approaching him, and they went their separate ways.

While at the park, Tara would make a trip to the restroom but because she was still learning her way around, she didn't know where to go. Franklin happened to be heading to the restroom at the same time and asked if that is where she was going. When she said yes, he graciously volunteered to show her the way. As Tara came out of the restroom, Franklin was waiting and asked her if she was "socializing" with anyone. Tara says it took her a minute to understand what he meant by "socializing," but when she realized he was trying to *holla*, she said, "No, I'm not socializing with anyone." At that moment, Franklin escorted her back to the park.

For the next hour, Tara and Franklin would engage in conversation and ask one another lots of questions. They laid all their cards on the table. Tara asked if he had kids, and he said no. She smiled with excitement at this news. She said he kept complimenting her but never addressed her green eyes like most people had in the past. She said he had great attention to detail about the things that attracted him to her. She appreciated that about him. At some point, Tara realized she had forgotten all about her girlfriend, whom she had left alone. She then invited Franklin to join them.

The next day, Franklin expressed to her that he wanted to call her after the concert but relented to save his excitement. Tara said she had looked online for questions to ask Franklin, as she felt that a lot of people enter into relationships without asking the questions and later regret their choices. So when they conversed, they asked each other the tough questions. This would continue for a while.

On their first date, they went to Dave and Buster's. Tara said she noticed that he stood at the door and opened it for her, which he continues to do still to this day. Because of their work schedules and the living distance between them, Tara and Franklin would only see one another twice a week, unlike most couples who see one another every day. They would alternate planning dates for one another. This encouraged them to take an interest in something that the other person liked. She would plan a date that included something he liked, and he would plan a date with something she enjoyed. They would always make sure it included a game night and never the same game night to keep their relationship fun and spicy. This would go on every week, usually on Thursdays and Saturdays with some flexibility for switching it up on Thursdays, so her girlfriends knew that Saturdays were his time.

One date night at the Dallas Museum of Art (DMA), Franklin asked Tara what was important to her in a relationship, and her response was intimacy (their code word: fellowship). Franklin responded that he didn't fellowship and had been waiting for some time. He informed Tara that he was planning to wait until after he was married to fellowship. So Tara asked, "So, no touchy-feely, only kissing?" And Franklin responded with an affirmative yes. Tara told Franklin that she would have to pray about that because her love language (as she discovered through reading *The Five Love Languages: How to Express Heartfelt Commitment to Your Mate* by Gary Chapman) was physical touch.

After praying about it, Tara agreed to proceed forward with this endeavor, but she would have more questions about how they would get there. So they discussed what that would look like and agreed not to stay at each other's house late at night. So when they would go on a date, regardless of who was driving, they would drop one another off at the door and go home. Even in their kissing, they would stop if they felt it could take them further than where they wanted to go. They held each other accountable to not cheat their way through the process.

Only seeing one another twice a week really helped set some good boundaries with their waiting and was helping Tara learn how to get out of her own way when it came to God's leading. She said physical touch was her love language, so she would find herself irritated at times because she wanted to be affectionate. Although this was a very hard process for Tara, she loved this man and didn't want to do anything that would take him off his journey. She said that once they started the process and she started praying more and writing down their goals, it became easier and easier.

When they met, Tara was attending the One Community Church and after they visited each other's churches, Franklin asked Tara to join him at the Potter's House. The decision to join him at his church would continue her growth in learning to submit to his leading. At every point of submission, Franklin would be a gentleman by opening the proverbial door for her to graciously enter.

In July 2014, Franklin would propose to Tara at Addison Park, the place where they first met. Franklin and Tara decided to complete eight weeks of premarital counseling to help prepare them for marriage. They both discussed topics in their relationship like finances, communication, boundaries, and family. Having successfully completed their waiting process, they were married in April 2015. Tara says that she and Franklin still court one another and have continued their weekly game nights and planning dates for each other. She says that what she loves most about Franklin is his heart for God and how he puts God first in his leading of their marriage. She says Franklin shared that when he was chasing her, God told him what to do and how to do it. He would always suggest they pray about their relationship, and today they pray together every day before they leave for work and before they go to bed.

Franklin is a minister at the Potter's House and has a small business. She loves that he is a provider and can sell like none other. She says he goes to the grocery store, and she likes washing the cars. She's glad that they can embrace each other's likes and not make it a gender-role issue.

Tara says Franklin is so patient. Tara is more of the spicy, fiery one and less patient. Yet, through Franklin's patience, she is becoming more patient and has calmed down a lot. As an independent woman, she realized that some of her efforts in their relationship were a bit controlling. She says she struggled with submitting and was always telling Franklin how she could do it herself. She says it wasn't easy, but that she learned to focus on the heart of his effort. She said sometimes they may not get it right, but that doesn't mean we beat them upside the head with our words. She said, as women, we can kill a man with our words. She says it makes it a lot easier for the husband when we submit, and in return, it becomes much easier for us as wives. She says it's been a beautiful journey and a blessing to blissfully live out Proverbs 31.

Love in Action: Loving Through Courtship

1. Seek God for His best choice of a mate for you. Ask God to prepare you for His best choice and to give you wisdom for the journey.

2. As you're exploring your options for courtship and marriage, make the selection process a fun and honest excursion rather than a dreaded lock-down course. Three great resources are *Choosing God's Best: Wisdom for Lifelong Romance* by Dr. Don Raunikar, *Lies at the Altar: The Truth About Great Marriages* by Dr. Robin L. Smith, and *Temptations of the Single Girl: The Ten Dating Traps You Must Avoid* by Nina Atwood.

3. As God blesses you with the desires of your heart, create awe-inspiring, lasting memories and delight in the beginnings of a lifetime of His greatest love!

CHAPTER 19:
LOVING YOUR SPOUSE

Wives, submit to your husbands as to the Lord. -Ephesians 5:22

Husbands, love your wives, just as Christ loved the church and gave Himself up for her. -Ephesians 5:25

ALTHOUGH I HAVE NEVER BEEN MARRIED, I'VE HAD A front row seat to some really great marriages as well as some not so good marriages. As a result, I have gained great insight through their experiences. Some of the most amazingly impactful biblical teachings on marriage I've learned from my founding pastor, Dr. E. K. Bailey, and his wife, Sheila, and my senior pastor, Dr. Bryan Carter, and his wife, Stephanie, of the Concord Church in Dallas, Texas. Through the transparency of all of these relationships, I've come to know the makings of a lasting, loving marriage and the commitment required for longevity. I don't purport to know everything, but my hope is that you will be open to the design that God intended: marriage for a lifetime and love unconditionally.

Marriage is what you make it; give it all you got! If you make it a source of contention, that is what it will be. But if you make it a breeding ground for real love, you become a channel for personal and spiritual growth. When you say, "I do," you become one flesh.

As that one flesh, you must honor one another as you would yourself. You must go into marriage with realistic expectations yet unconditional commitment and devotion.

Relationships can bring out the best in you, or they can bring out the worst in you. The height of your relationship will be determined by how you are invested. Make a wise, low-risk, high-yield investment, and you will gain steady long-term returns. A foolish, risky investment will result in a volatile return on investment (ROI). Whatever the option you chose, be prepared to live with it and be welcomed into the investment club of happily ever after!

Consider the Order

In order to have a successful covenant, you must sustain the order of your marriage. God must be the first priority! To know true love, you must know the One who created love. You must have a relationship with Him and grow in that relationship. Then you must learn to love yourself. The love you give to yourself is likely to be the kind of love you will give your spouse. If you give good love to yourself, your spouse will reap the benefits. If you don't take care of yourself or always focus on the critical, your spouse will likely be miserable. If you are not whole going into the marriage, it's probable that you will be looking to your spouse and not God to establish your wholeness. Please know that it is not humanly possible for your spouse to do that for you. Your spouse can add a certain depth to your life, but he or she cannot fulfill your God-given desires because he or she is not God.

One of the biggest mistakes couples make is that they look to one another to fulfill their deepest desires. Let's think about that for a minute. Remove your spouse from the equation for just a moment. Fulfilling your hopes and dreams takes not only faith, but also a great deal of work. Realizing how much effort that is for you to do for yourself, why would you expect someone to do and be that for you? That is a HUGE responsibility! Instead of looking to your spouse, you should be looking to God to fulfill all your hopes and dreams.

Not only that, God is a jealous God and commands you to not have any other gods before Him. So, look to God to be God and your spouse to be your protective covering for a lifetime. Then, and only then, will God allow your mate to be a conduit for His blessings.

Learn How to Stay

Don't expect perfection! Don't mistake shifts in your relationship to mean something negative like "falling out of love." Where there are relationships, there will be challenges. Bottom line. Why? Because relationships are made of imperfect people who will never do things perfectly. If having problems in your marriage means that you married the wrong person, then everyone made a poor choice in selecting their life partner. When you see couples whose marriages have sustained a half century or greater, don't you ever question what has been their secret? Do you think they never had any major problems in their marriage? If you were to sit at their feet and listen to their stories, you would realize that they not only had challenges, but real problems...not some of the surface-level things that some couples fight over (and name it "irreconcilable differences") that really have nothing to do with anything. Actually, most times, those long-lasting marriages not only had worse problems but went through more challenges. One great wisdom that our grandparents were able to reach that so many of us have never experienced is they learned how to love unconditionally. They learned how to stay.

Love is a gift. You don't have to give it or receive it, but if and when you do, it will bless you. Still, it will hurt at times: hurt is just a process of refinement. When you exercise, there will be muscles that ache in those areas that haven't been worked out. And until that muscle is conditioned, the pain remains. If you quit, you'll have to start over and endure the pain again and again until that muscle has been strengthened and your endurance improves. When it reaches that next level, pain comes yet again to make you stronger in that new season.

Exiting is easy. It takes an amazing strength to know how to stay. God gives us free will to choose so you can leave if you want; but at the end of the day, you must still get the lesson. The battles you're constantly having are a result of your ability to allow the enemy to stand in the gap of your marriage rather than allowing God to make you uncomfortable so He can grow you in those areas. You can choose to make it about your spouse and seek love elsewhere. Even if you get a new spouse, the lesson will stand until you get what it is He's trying to develop and mature in you. Water your own grass. Where old love has died, new love can grow.

Let Go of the Conditions

Whether you believe it or not, love was created to be unconditional. To attain real, lasting love, you must let go of the conditions. Conditions are contractual and have to be met before I will love you. Loving with conditions is like doing business. When business is good, everyone is usually happy. When business starts going south, attrition is likely, and people can feel that and see the writing on the wall.

Unconditional love is choosing to love before and after you have said I do, even when things may be going south. It doesn't mean that you let the Mr. or Mrs. harm you in any capacity. Anything that causes detriment to one of God's children is not acceptable love. Unconditional love says that regardless of whether you choose to go all in, I will go all in. My ability to love you at the highest form of love is not dependent upon whether you love me at the highest form of love.

In marriage, conditions are merely lies of the enemy. Don't buy into the lies. They will show up in your disagreements and frustrations. They will show up as high expectations and disappointments. Conditions are the enemy's MO for pitting you against one another. Every time you submit to them, he wins. Unconditional love is possible. You simply have to learn how to give it.

Communication is 100 Percent Critical

Effective, open communication is 100 percent critical. Breakdown communication and seemingly all other lifelines begin to unravel. To effectively communicate, you truly have to want to hear what is on the other person's heart. It's hard to communicate when no one is listening. And to listen, you must rid yourself of the pointless distractions and be attentively present for the moment at hand. Resist the urge to put off your spouse when he or she is in midsentence about a matter that is focal. When you unnecessarily interrupt, it says, "Although it may be important to you, it's really not important to me." If the mission is to enjoy a simple evening at home watching the game together, chalk the constant desire to be anywhere but present. Put the interruptions away and focus on what is in front of you. Kill the distraction addiction.

Make an effort to establish a deep connection through one-on-one, face-to-face, eye-to-eye linking. The purpose of communication is to deliver a message while establishing an unfathomable human connection. It's a message to say, "I love you. I appreciate everything you do for the life of our family." Or it says, "When you say A, it makes me feel like B." When the message we send out is received with mutual love and understanding, that connection not only deepens but also strengthens. We don't always get it in the moment; sometimes it takes stepping away from the conversation to take stock and see the matter from the other person's perspective. When you communicate, don't ask questions to back the other into a corner and then attack. Ask questions to gain understanding. Then, take the insight you've gained, and implement a solution that improves the condition of your relationship. More than anything, shower your spouse with compliments and appreciations of all you love about them and less about what you feel they don't do right.

Communication should be enjoyable. You should look forward to connecting with your spouse. It should be fun and refreshing. When you communicate with him or her, you should want to leave them better than when they came. You should be able to learn novel and stimulating ideas from one another. Your communication should help one another grow. Because it takes two to communicate, make sure it's always good on your end. You can't control how another person will respond, but you can at least give it your best energy, your everything.

Communication must be honest. And to be honest, both parties have to be vulnerable enough to trust the other person with his or her truth, putting down the fight to be right. Truth can sometimes be tough to give and receive but necessary if you want to go deeper in your relationship. If you present the truth with a level of consideration and sensitivity from the other person's vantage point, you can score the majority of the time. A good method is to always start with the positives, then introduce the truth or concern and end with the positives. However, if the truth you're presenting is intended to hurt the other person, they will likely remain in shallow waters and avoid risking going out too deep with you.

In your marriage, your communication must be between you, your spouse, and God. There will be times, maybe even many times, when your spouse will do something that frustrates you. And that's okay. What erects walls in your communication is when you don't address it with God and your spouse first. When your first order of business is to use the communication exit door and consult with your boys, fraternity brothers, and/or your "play sister" about your wife, it can infuse the flames. Complaining about what she isn't doing right or how crazy she is to others says more about you than her. The same applies to us women. We have to stop the "venting" to our girls and/or homeboys about our man.

If you're going to seek counsel, do so from wise counsel who has what you're trying to achieve. At the very moment your mate does or doesn't do something that is not in line with your expectations, kneel and talk to God about it. Don't make any hasty decisions without first talking to God. If you're in the heat of a conversation, it would be wise to ask your spouse for some time to think about the matter. Refrain from the temptation to share your frustrations with others. Consider what you've contributed to the frustration. Are your expectations unrealistic? Are you communicating to your mate that he or she isn't enough? Does he or she feel unloved or controlled? As you ask for His guidance, be quiet and listen to His instruction. It's amazing how God will change you as He's fixing the situation. Whatever He says to do or don't do, be obedient. Remember you're on the same team. Always assume that anything said by your spouse was not made with ill intentions or to harm you and roll with it. If it's a repeated offense, then determine the weight of the concern and whether it's even worth addressing. It may be just who they are; don't make it a personal matter. If you're going to fight anything, fight to stay together. Stay focused on the war to win in your marriage.

Don't Try to Change Your Spouse

We were all created uniquely by God for a purpose. There are no two people perfectly alike in its totality. So to attempt to change your spouse says to her that she is not enough as God crafted her. There is a fine line between encouragement and a demand for change. Encouragement says you are great and champions you to continue to do even greater things. A demand for change says you have a long way to go; and in fact, I'm going to remind you, at every point, where you are until you get to where you're going. He or she doesn't need to be constantly reminded of your preferences or what you don't like. Change can show up in your conversation, from out of nowhere it seems. You could be in a wonderful mood and be talking about the sun being orange and how you love the orange sun. Change will say that you need to see the sun as yellow; it's not orange. Until someone has walked in your shoes, it's all perspective. The sun being orange is not wrong but trying to control every minute detail that someone says or does in the relationship is wrong.

Your husband or wife is who you married. They may have grown in different respects; but at the core, he or she is who you stood with at the altar. Your spouse will value things differently than you do and vice versa. What's important to him or her just may not be important to you, so don't force your values upon one another. Accept them for who they are, but love them enough to share in some of the things that are of importance to them. Their love language may also be different from yours. The key is that you establish solidarity on which to build your house and the commonalties that make that house strong. Then learn to decorate your home with those differences. You might be surprised how beautiful the home can be with the unique art of the other's impressions. You have to learn to love a person for how they want to be loved, not how you think they should be loved or how you want them to love you. Get caught up in speaking their love language, not just for a season until you get what you want, but for your natural life as one.

Stop Speaking Divorce

Stay married long enough and you will start to believe you married the wrong person. What you perceive as insurmountable differences, God intended to build your character and deepen your relationship. But if you're so focused on happiness, you'll be blinded by your own selfishness. If you will allow the disagreements to make you better, you will draw closer to one another and create an unspeakable intimacy. However, if you keep looking at your differences for what they are not, then you will soon drift into the wind.

If you want to get a divorce, then all you need to do is keep dangling that word in your spouse's ear. Words have amazing power. I would encourage you not to use that word in your marriage. What you speak, you give life to. Use your words to speak life into your marriage. When your spouse is at his or her worst, love harder. Fight for, not against. Surrender your back-up plans and selfish desires.

He or she is not the enemy. His word says we wrestle not with flesh and blood but with the principalities of this world. The enemy has pitted you against one another, and you've fallen for it. Take your relationships back. Love. Forgive.

If you're going to stay in the marriage, make it count; don't do it halfway. Why would you want to live your life as anything less than the greatest each and every day? If you have children, don't just stay in the marriage for the kids. They will see you operate in half, and that is what you will teach your children: how to have a mediocre marriage. Unless they come to know better about marriage, that's what they will give their own spouse: half effort. And don't be surprised if they come calling you about their spouse and what's not working out. You will likely encourage them to do the same thing you did for your marriage: exit when the kids are gone. Your kids deserve better, so give them a healthy model of marriage. They see and take in every fight you try to hide. They see mommy when she cries. And they see when dad stays away because he just doesn't want to deal with the stress. Your kids will carry all of your burdens in their spirit unless you show them better. So get back in the game but go all in this time; go into the zone. Let nothing and no one tear apart your marriage, not even you. Instead, focus on the win and bring home a championship.

For the Love of Money

Money is a resource. It's a means to an end. It was never created to be worshiped, only managed. When you love money more than your spouse or badly administer your wealth, it can become a costly undertaking. One of the root causes of divorce is the conflicting views on money, so ensure you understand and embrace one another's position on money. You can't afford to allow it to become a wedge between the two of you. Matthew 6:24 says, "No one can serve two masters. Either he will hate the one and love the other...You cannot serve both God and money."

We are called to be good stewards over the resources entrusted to us. As a couple, determine how you will allocate your income and make wise spending and saving decisions together. Safeguard God's mission as a priority of your benevolence. Give generously, as money was intended to be kept in the flow. And don't forget to make the all-important love deposits.

Do Not Withhold Sex

God made sex, and He made it good! He made it to be thoroughly enjoyed and explored under the covers of the marriage covenant. He established sex as the ultimate gift of connection and deepest level of intimacy. Unwrap His gift! Revel in it in all its miraculous wonder as He designed it. Celebrate your love, and glorify the Father who is in Heaven! Your passion and pleasure will make the angels blush.

Conversely, when you reject your spouse's desire to make love, it can formulate an equation for divorce. When a spouse goes on a sexual diet, it mentally damages the intimacy of your relationship. It creates an action and a reaction, a cause and an effect. It constructs a HUGE question mark in the mind of the spouse who desires intimacy; it crafts an alienated mindset. That mindset renders a slew of derivatives, including a lack of self-esteem as well as anger and resentment. The lack of esteem derives a loss of passion and intimacy. It builds a doubt that questions, "Am I good enough for my mate? Is my woman attracted to me? Does my man enjoy sex with me?" The resentment and anger stirs the ego. The resentment will erect scorn and distrust, while the anger will cause dislike, disillusion, and infidelity.

"Marriage should be honored by all, and the marriage bed kept pure" (Hebrews 13:4). Don't use your gift of sex as a weapon; don't withhold it for self-centered reasons. Temptation is real, and the right temptation can trip you up even in the areas for which you think you are strong. For it's in those areas you've let your guard down that the enemy seeks to creep in. When you're feeling unloved by your spouse, it can seem right to explore sex elsewhere, but the enemy is crafty. Don't feed the lust. Simply walk away; take the opposing route.

Not only is love not a feeling, but His word explicitly said that sex was to be between a husband and his wife, no other. "Each man should have his own wife, and each woman her own husband. The husband should fulfill his marital duty to his wife, and likewise the wife to her husband. The wife's body does not belong to her alone but also to her husband. In the same way, the husband's body does not belong to him alone but also to his wife. Do not deprive each other except by mutual consent and for a time, so that you may devote yourselves to prayer. Then come together again so that Satan will not tempt you because of your lack of self-control" (1 Corinthians 7:2–5).

Don't let the fire die; keep it ablaze. Honor the Father by accepting His love. Share that love with your oneness, and "become in his eyes like one bringing contentment" (Song of Songs 8:10).

Court Each Other Still

Even after the marriage, continue to court one another with a greater level of intensity as when you first met. Greet each other with passionate affection. Often revisit the places where you first professed your love. Take the walks in the park, the trips, and the dinners out. Continue to intrigue each other. Support your respective hopes. Don't take each other for granted; make one another a priority. Don't stop gazing into each other's eyes. Be spontaneous and lovingly surprising. Create new, lasting memories on which to draw. Act as if each time you depart from one another's presence it will be your last.

A Marriage Made in Heaven

The love story of Jacqueline and Edgar started when their paths intertwined by the help of Jacqueline's precious uncle, Rev. Gregory Jones. The two met on September 2, 2001 at Ebenezer Baptist Church in Starkville, Mississippi. The church was the place they first met, and ironically, it would be at the church where they would secure and finalize their love for one another.

The way Jacqueline's uncle, Dr. Jones, introduced them was uncommon to say the least. He introduced them by looking into Jacqueline's eyes and proceeded to say, "Jackie, this is Ed, your future husband." Then he looked at Edgar and said, "Ed, this is Jackie, your future wife; now, go and make that happen." Needless to say, both Ed and Jackie were blushing and somewhat embarrassed by the bold way he introduced them, but it broke the ice, making those awkward first meetings a little more bearable.

Jacqueline coyly asked what he did for a living and other basic, get-to-know-you questions, and as he answered, she tried desperately not to show how smitten she was over him, as well as trying to quiet the loud voice in her head saying, "THIS IS THE ONE!"

Shortly after their first encounter, Edgar and Jacqueline's relationship quickly grew into a friendship that transpired over the phone, as he lived in Atlanta and she resided in Dallas. The marathon phone conversations that so often spun early into the wee hours of the next morning were not enough, and they began to plan trips to see one another every month.

Their relationship swiftly moved from a friendship to a courtship, and on December 31, 2001, Edgar professed his love for Jacqueline, and they would bring in the New Year as boyfriend and girlfriend. Soon after they both professed their love for each other, Edgar felt it was time for his mother to meet the object of his affection.

In February, Jacqueline flew into Atlanta to spend Valentine's Day with her sweetheart. It was during that trip that Edgar decided he would take her to Jackson, Mississippi to meet his family. Edgar received his family's blessing and knew the writing was on the wall that this courtship was the beginning to spending his life with what he knew was the love of his life.

The day Edgar proclaimed his love for Jacqueline to her family was Easter weekend of 2002. On March 31, Edgar got down on one knee and asked Jacqueline for her hand in marriage. Jacqueline, without hesitation, said yes, and on December 14, 2002, they wed. The ceremony and the weather were beautiful, which they both felt was a sign from their Heavenly Father that this union was destined by Him.

After almost thirteen years of marriage, they feel more in love than the day they first met on that rainy Labor Day weekend in Starkville, Mississippi. They say the success of their marriage has primarily been because of eight things:

- We have a relationship centered on Christ. We both value our faith, and it is by far the most important thing to us besides our precious children. We pray together, go to church together, and encourage one another through God's word. We value the commitment made to one another because we value our commitment to God.

- Investing in our marriage, whether it be participating in couples' workshops and studies or reading books together about strengthening our marriage.

- Dating and courting one another. We make it a point to spend time together, if it's going dancing or watching a good old movie or sometimes a basketball game (NBA finals) snuggled up on the couch. Keeping our friendship a priority has been vital to our marriage. We are friends, and because friends like to hang out and do things together, they make time for one another, so why not make time for your best friend, which, in our case, is our spouse.

- We make each other laugh. We love to find ways to get the biggest laugh from one another. If he or I see something that cracked us up, we are both like, "I can't wait to share that with my wifey or hubby." It keeps the joy in our lives and keeps us balanced, especially when life gets tough with respect to raising our kids, paying the bills, and the demands of our jobs.

- We fight, or as we like to say, have "intense fellowship." We are not afraid to fight; and as God has matured us, we are learning how to fight fair and express our frustrations and/or anger in a godly way. We do not cower down from our feelings, as we are getting better at being transparent and letting each other know how we feel, especially when one of us has offended the other.

- Sex is less a duty or a dominate focus in our marriage as it has become an expression of our love for one another. We both care about satisfying each other's needs first; sex moves from just being a physical act to a deeper and more intimate emotional connection for us.

- Neither of us was a virgin when we met, but we decided to wait to have sex before our marriage. We feel because we chose to honor God with this commitment to abstain, it resulted in us having a bolder faith when it came to the promises of God for our marriage. It also communicated to each other that we were both so valuable to one another that we were worth waiting for.

- We established boundaries as it relates to our children and other family members and friends. We work hard to respect those boundaries (i.e., date nights, keeping our marriage business between us, holiday traditions for our immediate family, etc.) to accomplish healthy relationships both inwardly and outwardly.

Love in Action: Loving Your Spouse

1. Pray daily for your spouse. Two books on praying for your spouse that I recommend are *The Power of a Praying Wife* and *The Power of a Praying Husband* by Stormie Omartian. Very powerful reads!

2. There's a difference between setting unrealistic expectations and having a clear understanding. Choose daily to resist your selfish desires and unrealistic expectations of your spouse.

3. Love your spouse in the manner he or she prefers to be loved. Most importantly, love them without judgment; love them for a lifetime.

CHAPTER 20:
LOVING YOUR CHILDREN

These commandments that I give you today are to be upon your hearts. Impress them on your children. -Deuteronomy 6:6–7

MY HEART IS BIG FOR THE KIDDOS! AND I HAVE CARED for myriad children in my life. From feeding, changing diapers, and rocking an entire nursery of newborn babies to sleep to mentoring high school and college students, I've enjoyed loving on and serving every age. As others have heard the adoration in my voice for these children or watched my love in action, unsolicited, they have shared with me that someday I'm going to make a great mother. I surely pray so and welcome the miracle. Until that day, the encouragement that follows is shared from my experiences with the children I've known and loved and/or from the sharing of other parents. May the words imparted be a blessing to you and your children.

The love relationship you have with your child is naturally one of the greatest unconditional love experiences you will ever know. Even before you meet them, there is an unspeakable, innate love you have for them that is indescribable. It's also one of the best gifts you can receive from the Father. To be entrusted to love and care for this little person, that is a mini version of yourself, is a divine miracle to say the least. Just as the Father chose you to love, He allows you to inherit that same kind of love by your choosing to love your child in a way that only a parent knows how. Yet, if you love your child with conditions, you're going to have a very challenging parenting journey. Your love for your child must be unconditional, first and foremost.

Give Them the Gift of God

"Train up a child in the way he should go: and when he is old, he will not depart from it" (Proverbs 22:6 KJV). The best and most important gift a parent can give their child is a relationship with the Heavenly Father first and foremost. It's the gift that never stops giving.

How you treat them will be their first look into who God is. You allow them to get to know Him by sharing the stories of the Bible; they love the stories (smiling)! You show them how the lessons in the Bible apply in their own life. You explain to them what sin is and equally the grace that Jesus shared for sin. You teach the importance of the relationship and prepare them for the ultimate decision to one day personally receive God as their own Lord.

Give Them You

Give them you, a healthy you. Gift your child with your undivided attention and lots of love and understanding. With all the distractions that compete with your time, it can be a struggle to detach from the disturbances and be keenly present. Yet, make an intentional effort to do so, and give your child your best you. Make sure the time spent together is quality over quantity. You can spend a whole day with them in an activity yet never connect, or you can spend an hour of intentional time touching their soul in the places that matter most. Your time with your child will be priceless. You don't get a do-over should you choose to forfeit the opportunity to be there for them; you don't get a replay to get to know your child and your child to know you. Yet, God can do the impossible and provide a second chance, as well as provide healing and peace to move forward.

Get to Know Them

Your child is the greatest form of expression of yourself; he or she is a direct manifestation of your physical being as well as your inner self. So it comes to no surprise that your child will look like you and act like you in a million ways. Even with all the likeness, your child is still his or her own person. From the moment they are born, and as they grow into adulthood, there will be a uniqueness about them that sets them apart from anyone else in this world. You will need to spend time getting to know that person if you truly want to love your child. Spending time with them will require your total attention and focus. You will need to spend time in their world and on their level, connecting intimately. Allow them to show you the things they like. As you get to know them, celebrate their individuality and champion their dreams. Never put limits on what they can do. If what they dream or desire is something you've never imagined as possible, make it possible for them. Whether or not you were able to accomplish your own dreams, it doesn't mean your child will fail. Their dreams are not impossible if you believe in them. Additionally, don't rob your child of their dreams by insisting that they live out yours in lieu of their own.

You scar your kids by having favorites. You teach your kids so much about love with stipulations when you impart discrimination in the family. Be sensitive about favoring a child that, by the world's standards, is more handsome or prettier or the child that is skinnier over the child who has gained weight. Instead of investing into all of the children on the level he or she needs, you choose a favorite. Not only is it disheartening, but it's lazy parenting. It creates resentment with the siblings and exhibits to them that they're not enough and will likely never be enough. It teaches them that love has to be earned and is something that is possibly unattainable.

You can love each of your children equally yet raise them differently. How you raise one child may be different from how you raise the other. That doesn't mean you favor one over the other or that you love the other more, it simply means you've taken the time to know each of your children in his or her own likeness.

Being Their Role Model

Model what you want them to be. You are their mirror. Every move you make and every word you share, they are studying you. It is what they know to be honest. From how you comb your hair to how you talk to your significant other, they will say and do exactly what you do. When you tell your kids to do as I say not as I do, that just piques their curiosity more. What you do is the most truthful expression of yourself and what they will begin to mimic. The same is true with those whom you allow in your inner circle. Who you surround yourself with is often who you are, so how do you expect your children not to become what they see? If you're suggesting they not do what you do, maybe that thing you do needs to cease. If you don't like what you see about yourself, make a choice to work on it and be committed to the change. As you change, your children will see that positive swing in your life and begin to live it out in their own life. You owe it to them to be a healthy image they should model.

Allow Them to Be Kids

There is a fine line between helping out around the house and assuming adult responsibilities. Find a balance in teaching your kids responsibility and allowing them to have a childhood. Be careful about tagging the only child or most responsible child to fulfill responsibilities of an adult parent who is always away or not present in the home. If you're a parent in this situation, it's quite possible you're completely unaware that you're doing this to your child. If you create this kind of relationship between you and your child in their adolescent years, it's likely they will get real familiar with putting on that same cape into their adult years. Because your child loves you, they will feel a need to continue to help you out in that regard, even if they don't have the capacity to do it. Love your child enough to be there for them instead of them always having to be there for you. Show them some love; they didn't ask to be here, so lighten their load.

Be Patient

Like a caterpillar undergoing a transformation to become a butterfly, your child will go through a metamorphosis and will need your support through the process. At the caterpillar stage, your child's job is to feed…feed on your nurturing and care as well as your teachings and modeling. What your child receives at the caterpillar stage will have long-lasting impact all the way into adulthood. When your child is full grown, it reaches the pupa stage. This is when your child will transition to college or to the workforce to receive further growth and development outside of your rearing. The adult stage is when your child will be required to reproduce and gift back to the world. This is the point when your child may marry and have a family of his or her own; or this may be your child's purpose and mission.

As your child undergoes his or her metamorphosis, he or she will need your patience and love. They will let you know when they need more love. Sometimes the need will not look the prettiest. More love needed will often equate to more patience. Take notice to the pleas and find out what the petitions are about. Be careful not to diminish their desire or want to hurry a resolve in your favor. Make sure the child's best interest is upheld and kept safe.

Show Up for Them

Be your child's biggest advocate and learn to safeguard their dreams. Your child needs someone who will believe in them and encourage their highest hopes to fruition. They need someone to help quiet their fears and/or to know that one person always has their back. They need someone to share in their joys; they want someone to high-five at the end of each endeavor. They want that someone to be you.

When you're not an advocate for your child, he or she will find someone who will support them, and you run the risk of pushing them into relationships that may not be in their best interest. Don't leave that window open for them to have to seek out meaningful relationships elsewhere. Life is hard enough; don't contribute to any voids in their life.

Allow your child the freedom to express themselves and listen to them. Your ability to have healthy two-way conversations will train them for a lifetime. Never sitting down with them and giving your attention shows them that they're not worthy of such love. Children are impressionable. You want to create such a level of trust with your child that they feel comfortable coming to you about anything. There should be no topic that is off limits for them to discuss with you.

Gift Them with Both Parents

Honor your children by speaking well of the other parent (whether he or she is your spouse or ex). Kids are smarter than we give them credit for. They know genuine love and feel it when it's not genuine. When you speak ill of the other parent, you're teaching them how to dishonor their parent when they can't get their way. You will hurt your child's relationship with the other parent because you have led them to believe you are the good guy and the other parent is the bad guy. That's just wrong on so many levels. If your spouse or ex hurt you by choosing not to love you in the manner you desired, don't rob your child of that love from their parent. At the end of the day, give your child the gift of knowing the good things about their mother or father. It doesn't mean you lie, but you allow them to love them for the good they do versus criticize them for what they are still learning. I'm sure if they knew better, they'd do better. A lot of times, people do what's normal to them. What's been their reality may not have been your reality, but don't punish them for that. When you let go, you allow love to come in and heal and restore. Bless your child with two parents instead of one.

Don't use your kids as ransom with the other parent. If you're in the position of sharing custody of your child, the parent that is to pay child support may simply not make the payments, for whatever reasons. Don't punish your child by keeping them from the other parent as a result. The only time you should look at withholding visits is if the other parent is likely to do something to harm his or her child. At that point, you're protecting them; just don't use your kids to be vindictive. Don't put the kids in the middle of your grievances. Together or not, one of the greatest joys you can give your children is parents who are at peace with one another.

Disciplinary Action

Speak to your children; don't yell or scream at them. Talking is just as effective. If you're responding out of emotion, hollering typically follows. Even if you yell and still allow them to get away with the very thing you're yelling at them about, they will just see you as emotional or not really meaning what you say. You can crush your child's spirit with such an emotional response. Don't rob or strip them of self-expression. It is greatly crucial that you give yourself some time to respond to the matter versus reacting.

Before you take any disciplinary action with your child, I encourage you to know all the facts. It's important you, as the parent, know and understand why you are disciplining him or her. Is it their behavior that needs to be corrected? Was your child doing something to harm himself? Or were you simply having a bad day, and your child stepped into that space of your day? If there was some behavior that happened outside of your presence, do your due diligence with all parties involved to gain an understanding about what transpired. Spend some alone time with your child listening to his or her side of the story. Evaluate the different perspectives and come to a conclusion about a course of action.

Respect your child enough to speak to them about your decision to warn or correct. Use this one-on-one time as a teaching moment to educate your child about what they may have done that was good and what they can improve upon or not do in the future. Let them know the consequences for their actions. More importantly, make sure your child truly understands why they are being disciplined. There should be guidelines established so that your child has some level of expectation that when he or she does A, the consequence is B.

Don't waste haste in disciplining your children when you see them going astray. "The rod of correction imparts wisdom, but a child left to himself disgraces his mother" (Proverbs 29:15). The key is that you establish correction at the time of error. Be careful though not to misinterpret what the verse says, as some will translate the verse to mean that you must beat your children, but His word says "the rod of correction," or discipline, which means to correct them when you see them heading down a path that does not and will not serve them well. Please be mindful of the enemy's craftiness in terms of this verse.

The kind of correction you give may be different for each child and depend on age and personality. As you learn each of your children, you will learn what works best for that child. Timeout may not work for Mason, but a conversation with him about how a leader conducts himself may be the encouragement he needs for self-correction.

Correct in private, never in public. You dishonor your child and can kill their spirit if you speak negatively against them in front of others. God smiled on you when He entrusted their very life to you, so honor Him by honoring them. Don't scold or ridicule your child but respect him or her. True enough respect is earned, but how does your child earn something they know nothing about unless you model it for them. Make sure that you're focusing on the behavior and not criticizing your child or calling them anything other than the name you bore.

Be a Village

I love family. And in my family, there is quite a number of us. However, I believe we can sometimes manifest false notions about what parenting and family is. I've always wanted to be a mother and have a large family of my own. Yet, despite that desire, it seemingly had not realized itself until God whispered otherwise.

A few years ago, I was blessed with a tiny surprise and one of the highest compliments I have received in this life. My best friend and brother-in-love gifted me with a priceless gift by asking me to be a godmother to their son, Kamdon. He's so adorable and perfect in every way. His favorite word to me is "no," except when it's time to sing a song; yet, his no's don't change my love for him. I love his giggles and the pitch in his voice when he means business. He keeps me smiling and my heart aglow. His big brother, Christian, equally stirs my heart. I claim him as my godson too. Christian is so full of life, and his smile could calm an ocean. He will have you buying him the world with those cute dimples. Without fail, when I hear him excitedly shout, "Aunt Jacquie," his joy makes my heart complete.

Yet again, God smiled my way and sent encouragement for the future. Many years ago, I committed to supporting a foster child in Zimbabwe named Trymore. After some time, he would complete the program, and we lost touch. Thanks to social media, and to my amazement, he recently found me online. He introduced himself as my foster child and shared that he now has a family of his own. I was overwhelmed by this unbelievable reunion. He now lives in South Africa, and we are making plans to meet for the very first time, God willing.

There are so many kids who need love and family. The love given to a child can come in many forms. Don't let a narrow view of family cause you to miss the inextricable blessings that are staring you right in the face. You never know what God is calling you to be in support of a child, so when the door of opportunity opens, make every moment count. Be a village.

God's Gifts

As I previously shared, life doesn't always happen as you planned it. The hopes and dreams you had for yourself may not have revealed themselves in the way you envisioned, but God can change the course of your life when you surrender to Him. God can resurrect the most unresponsive dreams if you stay in faith. "The Lord blessed the latter part of Job's life more than the first" (Job 42:12). For Kyle and Vanessa, they became very intimate with knowing this truth.

Kyle and Vanessa's Story

My husband and I met in college, actually my first day on campus, and we have been together for twenty-one years. We were married one year after our college graduation. Our plan was not to have children until we were settled, meaning owning a home. Our plan was structured well; however, we did not seek God's direction prior to creating the plan. We were settled in our home for two years and did not understand why we could not have children. After much prayer and seeking God's face, adoption became a consideration. God had equipped us with the resources, health, and strength to provide a loving home. However, before exploring that option fully, we scheduled an appointment with a fertility specialist. Two days before the appointment, we were informed of our pregnancy. During the pregnancy, we experienced some complications, and our daughter was born four weeks early but healthy and beautiful. Although we wanted another child, we were grateful for (the gift) the blessing God gave us.

After my aunt's passing and witnessing my cousin struggle with grief as an only child, we decided to seriously pursue our options to enlarge our family. We began to visit fertility doctors and were told we were both healthy and the reason for our infertility was unexplained. We were eventually given an option to try a procedure to increase our chances of pregnancy. After four years, we finally became pregnant again; but unfortunately, we miscarried. After further prayer, we revisited the vision God presented ten years prior and moved toward the adoption route to pursue a child in foster care. During the process, we faced many trials. My husband was diagnosed with cancer, my father's health conditions took a turn for the worst, and I was diagnosed with a liver disease. By faith, we continued to press through because we believed that adoption was God's plan for our lives.

We were eventually matched with six-year-old twin boys. Overall, the boys are awesome, considering the changes they have endured during their short lives. One of the challenges we faced with the boys was understanding, from their perspective, what it meant to be part of a (forever) family. We teach the boys the concepts of understanding unconditional love, the importance of discipline, truthfulness, and to respect themselves as well as others. We are learning to see and love the boys through God's eyes. We have been so blessed to have family, friends, neighbors, coworkers, church members, and teachers/educators in our lives that have accepted and been so loving to the boys.

Our pastor teaches that when walking in faith, you're called to do things that are not comfortable. So, we understand there will be peaks and valleys; however, with God's direction, mercy, and grace, we will continue to love and cherish the children that God has blessed us to parent.

Have Fun

At the end of the day, life is about living. Have family fun night! Play games together. Enjoy the happy moments and continue to strengthen your bond. Be the house clown for your kids. Make sure your time together is not all work and no play nor all play and no work. Let the kids plan an evening of enjoyment. Travel together and create positive, lasting memories. Most of all, enjoy one another and the journey, grow together, and stay together.

Love in Action: Loving Your Children

1. Pray regularly for and with your children. Pray for their salvation. Ask God to keep them safe from hurt, harm, and danger. Pray that God will grow them to be the man or woman He's purposed them to be. Pray that they will know love at the deepest of levels.

2. Create an environment where they feel safe to connect with you in the most honest way. Commit to being their protective covering and allow them to be their own best self.

3. Be present and seize the moments!

CHAPTER 21:
LOVING YOUR BLENDED FAMILY

Let no debt remain outstanding, except the continuing debt to love one another, for he who loves his fellowman has fulfilled the law. -Romans 13:8

IN 1969, THE TELEVISION SHOW *THE BRADY BUNCH* FIRST aired and became the go-to model for the blended family. It was the first stepfamily sitcom about a widower and his three sons uniting with a single mom and her three daughters. The *Los Angeles Times* reported that about 30 percent of families included a child from a previous marriage during the mid-1960s.

Statistics continue to show a steady growth of marriages that are resulting in blended families. A 2011 report, as a result of a survey conducted by the Pew Research Center, indicated that "more than four in ten American adults have at least one steprelative in their family." Of those same families, 70 percent expressed a great deal of satisfaction with their stepfamily.

Before You Say I Do...

Before you can truly love your future spouse, recognize that your love for your spouse's child must be unconditional going into the relationship. The dynamics of blended families can sometimes present a challenge, but on the same token, they can be absolutely gratifying. You have two families from different realities who are merging for the common goal of creating a family together. There will be issues that will arise—some as a result of the blended structure, and others simply as the natural progression of issues that would occur in most any family structure. How successful you are in building a strong family foundation will likely depend on how you start.

Start with lots of prayer and patience. Start by allowing the children to have some level of buy-in to the new life that will unfold. Even if you have already made the decision to marry, instead of announcing your decision to your kids, talk to them about what you're considering. Ask them about their feelings in the matter and listen attentively. If they celebrate your decision, praise God! However, if they don't, that's okay too. That doesn't mean you don't get married. Use that time to understand your child's sentiments and address any concerns they may have. Taking time to value your child's perspective will aid in their ability to make their own adjustments with the new family structure over feeling as though they're being forced to make concessions they may not welcome.

Keep in mind that there is a bigger picture in view. To attain blended bliss, everyone must commit to making it work together. Mutual respect and teamwork will be imperative for your family's success. More importantly, your ability to stand firm in unity as parents, as well as your modeling of a loving marital relationship, will be key.

You Set the Stage

As parents, you set the stage for the children for what love and family are. You will need to be their dream team. Your ability to make one another a priority and be a solid team will speak volumes to what the children accept or reject in the newly forming relationships. If they see a shaky foundation between you two, they know they can manipulate your bond (or lack thereof) to their favor. However, if they see you standing strong, they will eventually fall in line with your leading, even if done slowly.

It's Not Personal

The children of your spouse will likely have trust issues in the beginning. You may be viewed as a replacement of their other parent, which was a decision made for them and not one they have accepted. If the first relationship that involved their parents failed, they may feel like why get comfortable with the idea of this new person who is not their parent. In their minds, they already have a parent, so understanding your role may be a bit confusing. Not to mention, any type of relationship forged with you may feel as if they're breaking allegiance to the other parent. They may see your new relationship/marriage as cheating on the former spouse. As a result, they could very well see you as an intruder. No matter what transpired in their parents' marriage or contributed to the demise of the family unit, most kids still want to see their parents together. From a child's perspective, that's what they know to be family. That's what they know to be love…nothing personal.

Typically, in a blended family, the daughter is protective of her father and the son protective of his mother. Both will do their best to make sure their parent is loved always and likely attack in some manner if you remotely dishonor their parent. Doing so will prove that their feelings have been validated.

The children may also see you as a threat to quality time with their biological parent or fear losing that parent's love. You will have to balance protecting your unity with your spouse as well as managing their feelings of potential abandonment. So not only should you encourage their one-on-one, but you should also allow them that time alone with their parent and assure them that stealing their critical childhood years is not your mission.

As the stepparent, you will need to check your ego at the door and keep in mind that there is a bigger picture that has nothing to do with you. There are children who share in the brokenness of the family and may be carrying unwarranted guilt as a result. You may feel the need to exert your authority as the "woman/man of the house," but instead, take some time to get to know them and allow them to know you. Establish a nonthreatening environment where a relationship can forge organically between you and the child and naturally progress to mutual respect and understanding.

My father remarried when I was in college, so I didn't feel a need, nor have a desire, for another parent at that age. I think it was more difficult to accept a new family structure in my young adult years than if that formation had been made when I was a young child. However, through my getting to know my father's wife, she and I were able to establish a pretty good relationship that eventually progressed to a friendship. When it was time for me to sit for my CPA exam, her being a CPA herself was very instrumental in helping me study. In fact, since I've had my own business, she has been one with whom I've typically consulted when I had accounting or financial questions, and I am very grateful for the love she has shown me. As our relationship grew, so did my love and reverence for her as my stepmother.

If you're marrying someone who has a child, or children, and you have no children, often times you can feel like an outsider. If they already have their own routine, traditions, and a slew of activities, you may be wondering how to fit in, how to add value, or how you can help. You may struggle with feelings of alienation. This can be disheartening if you have always desired to be a parent and are feeling a bit invisible. On the other hand, always having to help out yet feeling unappreciated can also build up resentment. Regardless of the manifest, you have to know that this is what you signed up for. Take a page from the child's book and gain a different perspective. Recognize that greatness, like anything else, takes time.

Learning to Live as One

If you both enter into the marriage with children, there could be a whole new set of challenges, such as acceptance, sibling rivalry, and feelings of favoritism shown toward a stepsibling. First, accepting that there are real changes being made in their world (as far as family is concerned) may not be something of interest to them. Rather, they may feel, *If I don't acknowledge the relationship, just maybe it will go away.*

Having to learn to share time and space with any other child, particularly if that child is infringing upon their existing space, could provoke some discontentment. Although your stepchild may give you the blues or have nothing to do with you, doing something for your child and not doing something for them will give the perception that you love your child more.

As parents, discuss your parenting styles early on and come to an agreement about your roles with the children and how you will discipline. Balance those roles and disciplinary styles with the other parents who share custody. Determine how you will handle any conflict resolution with your children. Allow the children to have input into your new family blueprint and listen to their needs and concerns.

Adopting children is another type of blended family, particularly when you and your spouse have biological kids together. A benefit with an adoption is that there is typically an extensive amount of training and assistance provided to aid with the transition. Similar to marital blended families, there will be sibling rivalries and threatening feelings of favoritism. The biological children may feel like the newly adopted sibling is receiving more love, slack, and leniency than they ever received and possibly end up resenting you for it. On the other hand, the adopted child may feel like a stranger in your home and may build up anxieties. Fear of abandonment may dominate as they wrestle with adjusting to their new family. Making your newly adopted child feel safe and loved will be critical to the realization of your new family unit.

Whether through marriage or adoption, the husband and wife are the key to building a solid foundation for the family and protecting its unity. Moreover, keeping one another first while balancing the critical needs of the children is equally important.

All in all, blended families, even with the pronounced challenges, can be a miraculous blessing. As an adult child of a blended family, I see the love and expansion of our family as a gain. I've gained additional love and support as well as two older brothers and sisters-in-love. My nephews, Chris and Jaedon, have grown to be young men of such great character that it's a joy to call them family. My niece, Caela, is in a league all her own. There are so many similarities between the two of us, especially when I was a young girl, that I often refer to her as my Mini-Me. Although blended, at the end of the day, we're just family, and I wouldn't trade them for anything.

A Successful Merger

"Except the Lord build the house, they labour in vain that build it" (Psalm 127:1 KJV). Like most anything, what you build your house upon is what will stand. When Candace and Greg made the decision to marry, they knew blending a family would present challenges but were committed to establishing a harmonious union. As a result, they sought out wise, godly counsel. For them, the key ingredient to their success has been making God the head of their newly formed family.

Candace and Greg's Story
One of our goals with our union was to model a loving, Christian marriage. The children didn't have that previously. Our journey started somewhat smoothly, became a bit rocky, and is now smooth again.

We started the integration process by seeking GOOD godly counseling. We attended premarital counseling, which consisted of the following components: previously married, pastoral, and general, which included blended families that weren't previously married. We learned that, on average, it takes seven years to blend a family/form parental-type bonds. This helped tremendously because we weren't "rushed" to create this fantasy family. It was strongly emphasized to not let the children come in between the marriage. Everything needs to stay in His order: God, the marriage, and then the children.

Blended families can be capable of great unity, affection, joy, and love; however, it should not be entered into without much prayer and preparation. We have experienced the unique challenges of a blended family, as well as great love and respect. Along the way, we learned to celebrate the small victories. You have to be strong in who you are as an individual and couple in order to present a unified front to the children. It cuts down on trying to play one parent against the other. If they see a window of perceived noncohesiveness, they will stir the pot.

We agreed with that unified concept and had the biological parent ("bio-parent") as the primary disciplinarian, especially in the beginning. The kids, however, do understand that the stepparent has discipline authority given by the bio-parent. The kids' roles needed to be redefined, and new "house rules" were agreed upon and set forth in a family meeting. We learned to focus on what goes on in our house versus the other bio-parents. We emphasized that the new parent is an additional adult that loves and cares about them versus one trying to replace a bio-parent.

We have gotten through most of the obstacles with prayer and the following:

- Making time for the marriage through talk time, business time, and date nights.

- Deciding if the children's behavior is coming from a place of not knowing or disobedience. It determines the consequence and answers if it's a teachable moment. Don't take everything personally.

- Picking your battles, while still letting the other party know that they are loved.

- Agreeing to disagree and respecting the other's views. Realize that even bio-parents parent differently.

- Surrounding ourselves with other blended families.

- Spending time separately with each child or each parent with all of the children.

- Attending blending families' conferences and seeking additional counseling on blending.

- Knowing our legal rights for the best interest of the children.

There's a special kind of love to be shown, given, and absorbed in blended families, which makes all members better examples of God's glory.

A couple of resources that have proven to be invaluable and help beat the odds of divorce are *The Smart Stepfamily Marriage: Keys to Success in the Blended Family* and *The Smart Stepfamily: Seven Steps to a Healthy Family* by Ron L. Deal.

Love in Action: Loving Your Blended Family

1. Prayerfully, seek God for guidance on establishing your marital foundation before you say "I do." Even after the "I dos," establish a regular prayer time as a couple where you connect as three (i.e., God, husband, and wife).

2. Seek out wise, godly counseling that will help nurture and strengthen your family unity.

3. As the parents, set the stage and stand united. Most of all, turn up the fun and enjoy one another as a family!

4. As the stepparent, remember that great relationships take time and don't happen overnight. Make the unconditional investment to love your stepchild as if he or she were your biological child. Spend one-on-one quality time getting to know them and them to know you. Understand their love language, and surprise them with something you've learned that means a lot to them.

CHAPTER 22:
LOVING YOUR PARENTS

Honor your father and your mother, so that you may live long in the land the Lord your God is giving you. -Exodus 20:12

Her Children Call Her Blessed

Dear Mama,

Our Sunday mornings were filled with the sound of music...Shirley Cesar, The Williams Brothers, James Cleveland, and other gospel artists. You would rise early to shampoo your hair or sometimes prepare Sunday dinner. Other times, I wasn't sure why you were up so early because you would have awakened Chris and me to the bass of your favorite melodies. We would struggle to get out of bed, and I would have shampooed my hair as you had, gotten dressed, and was waiting in the den for you or impatiently running to and from your room to find you trying to finish your hair or put on those infamous "Dillard's" pantyhose (smiling).

It is those days that remind me so much of why I love Sundays and why I love you.

Matthew 7:24 states, "Therefore everyone who hears these words of mine and puts them into practice is like a wise man who built his house on the rock." You've been that wisdom for our family and have helped established a rock foundation of faith, hope, love, and family with a heart for God. I honor you for being L-O-V-E.

L—A LEGACY of love. You've always had our best interest at heart, even when we didn't think you understood. Whatever you did for us, you did it with par excellence. You taught me not to "straddle the fence." You said that good Christian girls don't party and try to sing in the choir too. Then, I thought you were being too strict, but although it has taken some lessons and some pain, I have finally come to understand. You weren't telling me I couldn't have fun, but that God wanted all of us and not just half of us.

O—An OPEN book and devotion for oneness. You have always been honest with who you are and have never apologized for it unless you knew it dishonored God. You taught Chris and I to cherish one another...you'd always say, "All you have is each other," and you made sure we stayed close. I can even remember you put us out in the garage once to settle a dispute. Once we thought about it, it seemed silly, and we quickly learned how to forgive one another. I think almost all of our family vacations were spent with family: Big Mama, Aunt Gladys and Uncle Tom, Grandma and Granddaddy, your brother(s) and/or sister(s), or cousins. Other times, you made sure we did fun things together like watching "family" movies, going to the park or zoo, or frequenting Mom and Pop's Snow Cone Place! I think your focus then has helped shape my continued desire to want to spend time with loved ones and get to know more of my extended family, no matter how imperfect.

V—A VIRTUOUS woman. "Worth far more than rubies...her children arise and call her blessed" (Proverbs 31). In the summers, you didn't have a lot planned for us to do, but you instilled in us discipline, as you'd say, "An idle mind is the devil's workshop." You said, "That hair better be combed, teeth brushed, and house cleaned by the time I get home." And we did...even if it was an hour before we knew you'd arrive (tee he he). And sometimes you caught us slacking on the job, and we learned from that; if nothing else, not to go to bed with dishes in the sink! You gave us a sense of responsibility by assigning us chores or paying a phone bill. You even let me exercise my entrepreneurial/negotiation skills when I told you I could wash and iron your clothes for twenty-five or fifty cents apiece versus taking them to the cleaners. You taught us to tell the truth no matter how much it hurt and that you may go easy on us if we did.

E—An extraordinary EXAMPLE of sacrifice. You would make sure you got to work early (i.e., while Chris and I were still sleeping) and make it home while the day was still young...most times shortly after we'd gotten home from school. You were committed to our after-school activities whether it was for practice or the actual game; you were there from tee ball, to softball, to track, to band...you ran. And you continue to give to Chris and I as if we have nothing, even when God has blessed us with so much. You've always been "a mama who didn't take NO mess" and had Chris's and my back at every cause, even if that cause meant you would go to jail for us...thank you! You made sure we didn't have too many priorities and kept the ones we had in perspective. So education was our job, as there was no working and going to school at the same time in your home. And I've come to value that and understand a person just can't do it all.

It is all these beautiful memories, lessons learned, and values instilled that I've become the woman I am today. For that, I am eternally grateful and forever changed for the better.

Mama, with all my love for who you are...here's to love eternal.

Love always,
Jacqueline (a.k.a., your Punky Brewster)

The Love...

There is something to be said about the fabric of a parent. Next to God, there is no greater love than that of your parents. From those moments when they kneeled next to you to say your bedtime prayers to teaching you all of the how tos—how to read, how to ride a bike, how to win—they were there. Of all the how tos, the greatest one of all was how to love. They cooked for you, labored for you, cared for you, and nursed you back to health. Through all the birthday parties and surprise moments, they were saying, "I love you."

No matter how old you grow, parents will still call you "my baby" and hug and kiss you like you're five-years-old. Even once you've reached adulthood, there is still probably nothing that they wouldn't do for you. Like a mother bear protecting her cub, they will go all in for you should anyone remotely look like they want to hurt the tiniest hair on your head. Whatever they have done for you and still do, know it is out of love.

Honor Them

Your parents made many sacrifices for you to make sure you had the best of everything and a richer childhood and life than that of their own. It would take a generation to repay them for all they have done. Although you will never be able to "out give" their love, you can pay them with the biggest compliment by honoring them.

There are so many ways to show admiration for your parents. You express reverence to parents by your submission to their leading and through the exchange of listening to their advice as well as being a listening ear for them. You honor them by helping and caring for them. Whether you send cards, letters, gifts, or whatever tugs at your heart, honoring them is just a way of saying thank you! All in all, there is nothing like a simple, verbal "I love you, and I appreciate you for all of you."

Stay Connected

In the days of our parents and grandparents, there was more of a close-knit family atmosphere where your neighbors were likely relatives or close family friends who became your village. They would help raise you and sometimes discipline you without prior authorization from your parents. As we have moved away from home, we've established our own lives, and those lives can get rather busy and somewhat disconnected. As we've gotten married, started careers in different cities, or even gotten sucked into the frequent business travel, it's easy to lose sense of that closeness that a family needs. No matter how far away you are, your parents want to hear from you. Even if they aren't the ones reaching out to you often or at all, they still want to hear from you. The joy I hear in my parents' voice when I call or share that I'm coming to visit does my heart good every time.

Continue to Get to Know Them

As time passes, we're all evolving. Prayerfully, the person you were yesterday is different from the person you are today, but for the better. We all must continue to mature and grow and explore the avenues God has laid in our path. The same holds true for your parents.

Even after all these years, I'm still learning new things about my parents. I love journeying back in time with them to the places they visited and experiences they had when they were young; those make me chuckle the most. If you take the time to ask them questions about how they were raised, you'll find out that most of what they taught you is what was taught to them. It helps you to see and understand the "why" in their story and cherish them that much more. More than that, you gain a greater appreciation for who they are and who they're becoming.

A Family That Prays Together, Indeed, Stays Together

A few years ago, a close cousin friend of mine shared with me that he prays with his mother once a week. I thought that was the neatest thing ever! I told my mother about it and jokingly gave her a hard time about why we didn't pray together regularly. That tug connected my mother and me as prayer partners. Then my dad and I became prayer partners, followed by my younger brother and me. Now, when my dad and I are praying across the miles, my grandmother is joining in. And when Grandmamma prays, you can feel Heaven smiling back!

Over the last few years that we've been praying together, I have seen God transform our family. As I listen to each of the prayers of my family members, my heart rejoices. My parents divorced when I was in the fifth grade, and seeing us all together now in harmony, supporting each other, laughing, and just having a good time stirs my soul. There is just something about praying for one another that opens a window to your heart. God never ceases to amaze me!

Forgive Them, for They Know Not What They Do

While others may have had really great childhood experiences, you might be saying yours was quite the opposite. Your parent(s) may have frequently been on the absentee or broken promises list. Or they may have been abusive and cruel and given you conditional love. They may have made your growing up a bad memory that you care not to revisit. Or rather you have no recollection of your mother or father because they abandoned you so many years ago. It's probable that with such experiences, you are now anxious about love and have repeated the cycle of conditionally loving with those in your own life. If so, I am praying for you.

Your mother or father may have failed you in their responsibility as your parent. Your feelings of inadequate parenting may be a result of cycles of broken generations. What was done to you is likely what was done to them. Although they may not have always, or ever, gotten it right in your eyes, know that they did the very best they could for you with what they had. Just as much as you want to be loved by your parents, know that they want to be just as much loved by you. Be the courage they need to take a step toward you. You thought they were supposed to teach you about love, but maybe you were brought here to teach them about love through your adoration toward them.

The best way to love a parent who wronged you is to pray over them and ask God to watch over them. Pray that God would align their hearts with His own. Forgive them for what they didn't or couldn't do by themselves. Love them anyhow out of obedience to God. They need your love above all else.

Take for example, Kendrick; he didn't grow up in an affectionate family. Hugs and kisses were practically nonexistent, and the words "I love you" were seldom, if ever, heard. When Ken got married and had a family of his own, it took the love of his daughter to show him a fresh way of loving his own parents. From the mouth of babes, she would tell her father she loved him and give him lots of hugs. Later, Ken built up the courage to express this newfound love toward his parents. After decades of lacking affection and not hearing his parents say "I love you," Ken now gets to hear and experience the love of a parent.

Rather, if you've never known your biological parents because of their leaving, find comfort in God's love: "Though my mother and father forsake me, the Lord will receive me" (Psalm 27:10). Instead of replaying a story of abandonment in your head, if your parent did anything right for you, choose instead to focus on that. Focus on what they gave you instead of what you believe they took away. You may view it as that they gave you up, but they may see it as they gave you to someone who could love you better.

Trust that God knows what's best for you. God chose your biological parents to birth you but blessed you with someone who loves you without comparison and beyond anything you could dream up on your own. God removed you from that former model to transition you to be more of who He needed you to be through a new model.

There may be a void in your spirit because you're looking for that someone that looks like you but consider the look of the inside of the heart of the parent who was or has been there for you. Maybe the void is not so much about the fact that your biological parent wasn't there for you and more about your own forgiveness toward them. Your parent leaving is probably the best thing they could have ever done for you.

A Father's Compassion

> Dear Daddy,
>
> I can remember when I was a little girl, and you took time to teach me how to ride my black bike with training wheels. And then you surprised me with a red ten-speed for my birthday...that was the best! You always had a special way of loving me, and I loved you in return for that. Although I love both of my parents immensely, I can remember as a little girl always wanting to go wherever you went. Going to watch you play basketball was my favorite. You played your heart out. You demonstrated that whatever you set your mind to, you can do with hard work and determination.
>
> Over the years, I've seen you evolve into the godly man you are today, still maturing and growing in Christ, as are we all. Although you practically live at that church serving as the head of this ministry and that, I know that it's not about the titles for you but your love for God. I remember

when you came to visit me in Toronto and seeing you reading and studying your Bible...that was life-changing. Whether you know it or not, it was that example of getting to know God through His word and the priority that you made it that started me on my own mission to know God more intimately. You've always been a good daddy and instilled in me many good values. You taught me to support the black community and to keep in contact with my former teachers and those who made it their business to encourage me in this journey we call life. You taught me how to make my own decisions and allowed me to grow in those decisions by not making them for me. When I ask for guidance, you give me godly direction through the wisdom and discernment you attained through studying God's word and through simply knowing Him. I've seen you overcome many obstacles, and I thank you for being more than a conqueror with all that life has presented you and for allowing me to see just how awesome God is.

Thank you for being protective of me and wanting me to be the best I could be. Thank you for being the kind of dad that gives of himself freely to help countless others in need. Thank you for teaching me the value of being on time and all that is worth. And thank you for covering my speeding ticket in college (smile), for the huge contribution after college, and for all the wonderful gifts (both tangible and intangible) you continue to shower my way. Most importantly, thank you for loving me unconditionally. Now and forever more, I wish for you all that God has for you! Your best is still yet to come!

Your loving daughter,
Jacqueline (a.k.a., "Jackpot")

Love in Action: Loving Your Parents

1. Pray for your parents regularly. Thank God for the gift of your parents and all they are or have been to you. Pray for their health and strength. Forgive them where they may have failed you.

2. Honor your parents by expressing your love for them through a spontaneously kind deed.

3. Prayerfully, write a letter to a parent who may have wronged you. Let them know you forgive them and hope they are okay. Whether you mail the letter or not, make sure you find a way to release that forgiveness into the world.

CHAPTER 23:
LOVING THY NEIGHBOR

*Greater love has no one than this: that he lay
down his life for his friends.* -John 15:13

MY FAVORITE PLACE BACK HOME IN NORTHERN
Mississippi was on the wooden swing of the front porch of
my Uncle Tom and Aunt Gladys's home. This home was filled with
so much peace that at night all you could hear was the stillness of
midnight through the raised windows and barely latched screen door.
Aunt Gladys was an amazing woman of God. She was the epitome of
love in the flesh, and I was drawn to her love like a moth to a flame.

When I was a toddler and was up walking, my mother said she
knew where to find me—next door at Aunt Gladys and Uncle Tom's.
She and Uncle Tom never had kids of their own, but they took care
of just about all the kids in our family. Her love was generously giving
but always firm. You couldn't help but have a deep reverence for her,
as she always spoke well of others and was always kind; I never heard
her say anything bad about anyone.

In fact, she stayed ready to love. Her table was always filled with
made-from-scratch everything, from breakfast to the most delectable

savory dishes and desserts. Although it was just she and Uncle Tom, you would have thought by the amount of food on the table every day that an army lived there. That wasn't the case at all; she was just a woman with a big heart for her neighbor. Everyone loved her because she loved everyone else. I can still feel her love till this day…

Learning to love your neighbor first requires knowing God and His love for you. Then we have to learn to see and love ourselves the way God loves us. God knew that without His example of love, we would not only be hard on others but could be equally hard on ourselves, at times our own worst enemy. How you love yourself and God is most often how you will love others. If you are one to take great care of yourself, it's probable you will do the same for others. If you make a mistake and beat yourself up because you believe God cannot possibly love you for that error, your love will likely be one of conditions leaving little room for mistakes. If you're hard on the other person for everything, you will reap a world of disappointment and hurt. God has standards for us and wants the very best for us, but He also knows we will stumble along the way and allows us to learn from those growing pains. He cheers us on to get back in the game and to keep fighting for the prize, which is the best relationship we can have with Him as well as building up His kingdom. We cannot build up if we're always tearing down.

Accept Others for Who They Are

The best love you can give your neighbor is the ability to be his or herself. Appreciating people for who they are is half the battle. We ruin relationships when we try to make others a replica of ourselves. God never intended for us to be the same or experience the exact same life encounters. What worked for you may not work for someone else. Just as some foods or medicines affect others differently, so it is true with experiences.

Learn to love people for who they are. When a person shares or exposes the truth about his or herself, accept it at face value. Don't try to make it anything more than what it is. Celebrate the best in others and share what you love most about them. If they're interested in your life, invite them in but don't confuse them accepting your invitation as a signed permission slip to seek to conform. Allow them to make the choice in how they will live their own life. Celebrate your differences and unique qualities. Don't try to be them, and don't make them try to be you.

You ask how you accept others when what they give you is a bunch of doom and gloom, nagging, and complaining. You pray for them. To pray selflessly for another person is one of the greatest displays of love. I say selflessly because we can have the tendency to want God to give us what we want. He says He'll give us the desires of our hearts, but our hearts have to be right with Him and with the right attitude, or He won't hear our prayers. You pray about how you are to respond to the place and period they are in.

The Friend That Is Always...

When someone stands in the gap for you, it says a great deal about their love for you. We all have a friend that is always something...always loving, always late, always helping, always cancelling, always calling, always...At least one of those "always" friends is you. Embrace the good and the not-so-good. When it's always good, enjoy it because to have one "always good" friend is a blessing, but to have many means you're favored by God.

If you have an "always not-so-good" friend, celebrate them too, as they need your love just as much. When they deal one of their "always not-so-good" moments, just smile. Why get mad about it? Recognize the source so you don't find yourself all roused about something that will never be in your control. Know that they don't mean any harm. That's just who they are and all they know to be. Love them too, as you also have something someone overlooks on your behalf!

A Die-Hard Fan

It's easy to be a friend when, as a team, you're on a winning streak, but should they go cold, please don't check out on them. What they are projecting is more about them than it will ever be about you. Although it feels like they are doing something toward you, and it may even be extremely exhausting, take a moment to look inside their journey and hear what they are really communicating to you. It's quite possible they are injured and having a hard time putting it into effective words about what that feels like. Although it may not make sense to you at the time, be a source of encouragement rather than of criticism. By no means am I suggesting you be a crutch or be a codependent to their pain. I do believe and know that sometimes helping others is not helping. Just as we must be patient that God will complete His work in us, we must allow Him to complete a work in someone else.

Resist the urge to rescue. That is God's job. He may have them in this season for good reason. If they are constantly asking you for the same advice but never taking any measures to correct anything, be lovingly honest with them about their cycle. Help them to realize they have come to you with the same request but have taken no measures to resolve the situation. Hold them accountable by not allowing them to come to you with the same request until they have taken some measure (even if it's not the advice you gave) to resolve, as they still must find their own way. When they make progress in their game, help them to celebrate the small victories. It will propel them forward.

Slow Down to Connect...You May Be Entertaining Angels

Slow down to connect. We strive daily to meet goals and objectives, but what are those dreams and aspirations purposed in? I think it's wonderful to excel at work, play sports, serve in ministry, and have a vision of attainment, but what we must not miss is the connections.

"Hi, how are you?"

"I'm good. How are you?"

"Good."

This is what you hear between strangers—brief encounters of pleasantries but busily not impactful. We're hurried to get here and there, there and here, but all the while we miss the bonding. Hebrews 13:2 suggests, "Do not forget to entertain strangers, for by so doing some people have entertained angels without knowing it."

I love it when a complete stranger takes the risk to go deeper and build an impactful connection. Really nothing else matters. God said you can achieve the highest mountain, but if you have not love, it profits nothing. Treasure the divine appointments. You never know, you may be entertaining angels.

The Woman at the Well

Every person is valued by God. How you treat others is how you treat God. How you love others is how you love God. He expresses, "Whatever you did not do for one of the least of these, you did not do for me" (Matthew 25:45).

God loves everyone. He died for everyone. Jesus hung out with the twelve disciples but He spent His life showing love to those we'd least expect. He showed love to the tax collectors, the lost, and the woman at the well. He was teaching us how to treat others even when the world said they're not deserving of such love. Take great care in how you treat others. You never know what a person is going through. The person you see as the life of the party may have simply learned how to be a professional at cracking jokes to mask his pain. The driver that just cut you off may be trying to get to the hospital in hopes of making it in time to say good-bye to a loved one. Regardless of the encounter, it pays to be kind to everyone whether you feel they deserve it or not. The person who is hurting the most will find a way to say it loud or become very good at hiding.

The woman at the well was so ashamed of where she was in her life that she went to one of the most social spots during a time she knew no one else was planned to be there. The Samaritan woman by the well (Jacob's well) was of a mixed race and was hated by the Jews. According to John 4, she had many husbands, and this fifth man (the one she was currently living with) was not her husband. Yet, God had a major love for her to be in a better place with Him and for herself. Jesus took the risk to love her and be seen in public with her in spite of where she had been and what she was currently doing. Verse ten indicates that the Samaritan woman was presented with a plan for redemption and resolve for her sinful life: "If you knew the gift of God." If God went in search of her to show her love for her worth, why would He not love you enough to do the same for you? As He was showing her His love, it created a desire in her to share that same love with others. If we are honest with ourselves, we have all had a woman at the well moment. God wants us to love everyone, even the Samaritan woman, even our enemies. His love ought to be contagious.

Breaking Barriers

We create big barriers, however, in relationships when we don't take the time to get to know one another. Getting to know someone takes going beyond the social experiment and creating purposeful, intimate relationships. As your intimacy develops, you create a safety net with one another where you feel comfortable sharing of yourself. The better you are at seeing your neighbor (and vice versa), the stronger the safety net you have. There is nothing more relaxing and freeing than being able to be yourself around another person and not having to explain yourself at every turn. When you're constantly felt misunderstood, there is a reason for that. Either someone isn't listening, someone isn't sharing, or both. Either way, the relationship doesn't permit you to go deeper because of the lack of intimacy and barriers in place. Friendship at its deepest level renders a love relationship that is mutually strong and lasting.

Standing Shoulder-to-Shoulder

We don't always get to choose our neighbors. Whether it's someone from your class project team, your job, or church group, God chose to put certain people in your life for your own good. This is often where we get our wires crossed. God's good and our good can mean two totally different things. Our good usually means, "As long as it makes me laugh or smile," while His good is concerned more about your character, your soul. While it's great to want to surround yourself with people you admire or have similar interests with, God is wanting to use you and bless you in return.

Jessica grew up working in the family business. She would spend her summers at the restaurant from the age of eight until she finished high school. During those years, her parents were positioning her and her brother to someday take over the family empire. As part of that grooming, her parents taught them first how to follow before leading. They also encouraged each of them to gain some key experience outside of the family business.

After high school, Jessica went away to college on the East Coast and lived in the DC metro area for several years. She returned home to Texas to accept the torch to grow and expand an empire that she hoped would someday serve her future family. Her parents had made great sacrifices to fulfill their dreams, and she wanted to honor the legacy of their sweat equity and love for their family. As a culture, Jessica also wanted to pass on more wealth (not riches) to the next generation.

As the family business required the daily attire of work uniforms versus a professional, stylish dress, this was not at all what Jessica had envisioned for herself. Yet, she would inherit a team of employees who had worked in the business for ten to twenty years, as they didn't have much turnover in the company. Some team members would expect certain benefits and perks as a result of their tenure. There was a high sense of entitlement with the team, so the announcement of Jessica as the new management presented many challenges for her.

Her team prejudged her position and wrestled with the change. Her dad told her, "The only person that likes change is a wet baby!" They viewed her simply as the owners' daughter as well as a spoiled brat. They misinterpreted her story and forgot all the summers she had contributed to the business. They further tested her will through attempted sabotage of things that had never happened in their business. From experiencing missing legal documents to no-shows and folks inputting hours they hadn't worked, they were on a mission to weaken her lead.

Instead of attacking back, Jessica elected to show love to her team through a shoulder-to-shoulder, "servant leadership" style. She says that you have to meet people where they are. She says that you don't lower your standards, but you meet people at a place where you're able to take them to the next level.

A woman of her word, she got in the trenches with them every day, some days eighteen hours at a time. As a result, she was able to demonstrate to her team that she was just like them. She said, "The only way to speak on it is to go through it. When people see you're with them, it speaks volumes. We're all in it together. We may be different, but we're also similar. It does not matter your race, last name, earnings, or where you're from. We're all going through something. In every testimony is a test. We must be supportive." She accepted people regardless of the differences and embraced the similarities. Through her leadership, she exemplified empathy with her team; they, in return, embraced her role as new management.

Love in Action: Loving Thy Neighbor

1. Ask God to show you how to love the totality of a person, not just the good.

2. Refrain from the temptation to try convincing someone of your way or change someone to align with your agenda. Take time to consider their "why." Agree to disagree.

3. Take a risk to go beyond your normal point of introduction and connect on a deeper level. What was that experience like?

CHAPTER 24:
LOVING YOUR ENEMIES

*But I tell you: Love your enemies and pray for
those who persecute you. -Matthew 5:44*

LOVING YOUR ENEMIES CAN ONLY BE OVERCOME BY
a deep love for God. God's love will unite you and break down
barriers of hate, judgment, and misunderstood lines where nothing
else can. Those who claim to love God yet hate or treat others with
disdain cannot fully love the Father.

How deep is your love for God? It must be really deep in the face
of opposition created by an enemy. I don't know any other love that
tests your obedience, self-control, and patience more than that of
loving your enemies. If you have enemies, know that you are doing
something right. If you don't have any conflicting opposition in your
life, you may be just where the enemy would have you—in a complacent state of coziness. If you are exactly where the enemy wants you
to be, he is at peace with you. Why? Because he has no need to test
you in something you have already attained. There would be no need
to create obstacles in your path or throw fiery darts at you because
you would be too busy working for him.

"But love my enemies?" you ask. "Why in the world would I want to do that?" He asserts, "You have heard that it was said, 'Love your neighbor and hate your enemy.' But I tell you: Love your enemies and pray for those who persecute you, that you may be sons of your Father in Heaven. He causes His sun to rise on the evil and the good, and sends rain on the righteous and the unrighteous. If you love those who love you, what reward will you get? Are not even the tax collectors doing that? And if you greet only your own brothers, what are you doing more than others? Do not even pagans do that?" (Matthew 5:43–47). With a command like that, how can you not want to at least try to love your enemies?

Don't Gloat When Your Enemy Falls

"Do not gloat when your enemy falls; when he stumbles, do not let your heart rejoice" (Proverbs 24:17). This is very convicting and can be a tough one to not entertain. How well you're able to say "no thank you" to rejoicing at your enemy's stumble says a lot about your heart and your love. Matthew 7:2 says, "For in the same way you judge others, you will be judged." Yeah, I don't want to be judged by God in that regard. Instead of expressing anger, show love and pray for those who persecute you. "Be imitators of God…and live a life of love" (Ephesians 5:1–2). Sometimes it's the people you least expect who will show up for you. So be open, and don't count people out.

Let Your Enemies Have Their Place

The key ingredient to loving your enemies is obedience. Because God is God, you have to know He has a wonderful sense of humor. I can't tell you how many times God has changed my heart when faced with an opportunity to love an adversary. It may be, by far, one of the hardest things you will ever do in your life, but for me, it's been one of the most worthwhile experiences. Each time I've submitted to God's way of loving, He has shown me Himself in the most unexpected ways, literally every time. What's even more beautiful is watching your enemies being transformed through your obedience and love for them. The people who have wronged me over the years, God has used them to usher me into my destiny on some level. Ask Joseph or Jesus Himself.

Joseph was forsaken by his brothers and experienced a great deal of adversity. His brothers' envy toward him was like no other. Their hatred had exposed the worst in them. They plotted to kill Joseph, thinking they could make him disappear and rid them of their hatred. Thankfully, God had a plan and placed it on Reuben's heart to save his brother's life. So instead of killing Joseph, they sold him into slavery. Even after being enslaved, Joseph encountered opposition after opposition that would have taken most people out. Yet Joseph rose to the occasion like a warrior. His faithfulness was rewarded by Pharaoh, who placed Joseph in charge of the whole land of Egypt.

After his father's death, Joseph was presented with an opportunity to be reunited with his brothers. He chose to forgive them and still expressed love to his brothers despite the mistakes they made. "But Joseph said to them, 'Don't be afraid. Am I in the place of God? You intended to harm me, but God intended it for good to accomplish what is now being done, the saving of many lives. So then, don't be afraid. I will provide for you and your children.' And he reassured them and spoke kindly to them" (Genesis 50:19–21).

In comparison, Jesus still showed love to Peter despite his denial. Jesus even foretold of his betrayal and allowed Peter's unfaithfulness to establish the precursor and foundation for salvation. It was all a part of the plan, and the sooner you are able to see the vision, the better able you are to pray for your enemies and be thankful for their role in your victories.

When the Enemy Is You

Sometimes your own worst enemy is you. It can be a tough reality to fathom when blaming is the name of your game. So the next time you're tempted to point a finger at someone, make sure that finger doesn't need to be pointing back at you. It takes courage and humility to admit a wrong and take responsibility for poor decisions. What's even worse than not owning responsibility for your actions is always assuming the responsibility for every mistake made by someone else. Always apologizing for something, especially when you've done nothing wrong, can be as equally unhealthy.

You will fail at times. You simply can't escape it, but let those failings tutor you and position you for your greatest coming. If you kick yourself while you're already down, it will make it extremely tough to see the horizon. You will never allow yourself room to grow by constantly criticizing yourself: "I messed up with A, or I hate I did B." Stop that! Please! The next time you have something of importance to do, whether it's speaking in front of the public or taking care of something entrusted to you, when it's all said and done, focus on the *many* things you did well and assess only a *few* things you can improve upon for the next adventure. Celebrate the victories and your journey. Choose joy!

Forgive Your Enemies

People can be cruel. They can want to see misfortune in your life for reasons unknown. When someone has wronged you, spoken ill of you, come at you sideways, hit you below the belt, or even left you with some pretty deep wounds, it can be tempting to want to see harm sent back their way. In your pain, you may be wishing they experience the very same kind of hurt they caused you. And to see them in a seemingly prosperous state after they cut you can be a hard pill to swallow. Being happy for them or wishing them well may be the last position of your heart. But if you don't get to a place of healing, their venom will poison you until you become just like the one who hurt you.

At the moment they chose not to do right by you, they stole away pieces of you. Don't you think they have stripped you of enough?

They have hijacked your time…time you can never get back. Let it go; let them be whatever they choose to be or go wherever they're going, but don't let them rob you by changing you for the worse. Matthew 10:14 states, "If anyone will not welcome you or listen to your words, shake the dust off your feet when you leave that home or town." Stop trying to settle the score with tit-for-tat efforts or by trying to get even. You do realize how much exhaustive energy it takes to hate someone and how much damage it does to your health, right? Choose your health over hate and peace over pain. Let the arrows they sent to destroy you grow you and transcend you. Whatever hurt you, ask God to allow you to forgive that hurt and the person(s) who inflicted the hurt upon you…even if that person has been you. A true test of whether you've forgiven is when you have no desire of looking back to the past; and when you see him or her, you have a genuine happiness in your heart toward them. Whether they realize it or not, not only do you need forgiveness for your own healing and joy, they need forgiveness, and surprisingly, someday you may find them thanking you for it.

Finding Peace

I had just purchased my first home. I had a bit of work I wanted to do before I officially moved in, so immediately I got to work. There were some clothes from the previous owner along with a file cabinet and desk mat that were left behind in the upstairs office. I contacted the realtor to have the clothes and other items in the office picked up. They asked if we would like to keep the file cabinet and mat, but said they'd come to get the clothes. My mother said she could use it, so I agreed to keep the file cabinet.

My best friend graciously volunteered to help me paint one wall red (in tribute to our sorority) around the living room fireplace and several other walls before the housewarming. In the month I was preparing my new home for move-in, I arrived home one evening to find a packet of molded bacon on my front porch. I thought it was odd. Clearly, someone was trying to send me a message, as that heavy packet of bacon surely didn't blow its way onto my porch. A bit of anger started to brew in my soul, but I chose to let it go.

We had just concluded an afternoon celebration for my house-warming and twenty-fifth birthday. Two of my closest friends, my mother, and I took in the night and sat around and talked. The front door was still open, but the storm door was locked. The doorbell rang to our surprise, and it was an elderly, fair-skinned woman. She walked bent over. We graciously greeted her in, as we had been accustomed to doing this April day. She introduced herself as my neighbor and pointed in the direction of her home and welcomed me to the neighborhood. I thought, "How very kind of her!" After a month of prepping the house, she was the first to comfort me in the neighborhood.

Completely blindsided at the time, that visit would be more than just a "welcoming." She asked me if I knew that the previous owner had died. I told her yes, I was aware. She then asked me if I knew how she passed. I said that I didn't. Antsy, she seemed she couldn't wait to tell me all the details. She informed me that the former owner was a CPA who was found upstairs. Apparently, she was working in the office when the industrial size file cabinet fell on her and contributed to her death. I was holding that same file cabinet in my garage (not good). Well, by the time this woman left my home, I was feeling a lot less celebratory.

I would later have more work done on the house; and every time I did, like clockwork, there would be some molded food or strategically placed trash of some sort appear in my mailbox, on my porch, flower bed, driveway, or yard. All things that couldn't just blow through the air.

Then, from out of nowhere, I got a call from this same neighbor one day that she saw someone jumping my fence as if it were a potential burglar on the prowl. When I started asking her details about what the person looked like, what did they have on, when did it happen, she had very little to no information to provide. I started noticing that she would contact me only to share things that might scare me.

I then started getting interesting reports from my contractors. Almost every supplier I hired would mention that my infamous neighbor would stop by each time and ask how much I was paying for the work to be done. They'd tell me they did work for her, and she didn't pay. She always seemed to be watching my bank account in regard to the house and wasn't shameful about the private information she was inquiring from me or my suppliers.

What was supposed to be a place of sanctuary had become a scene from the movie *Lakeview Terrace*. The trespassing and littering became intolerant, so I began to call the police each time it would happen so they'd have a record and history of each occurrence. I called lawyers about how I could handle the situation, but they said the only resolve was to catch her (the neighbor) on tape. I had suspected her for some time, and when I received a voice-mail from her that she was the one who had *inadvertently* stolen my trash can, I knew then I wasn't losing my mind. But, by law, it still wasn't the evidence I needed.

The neighbor would pop up often. This went on for years—talk about long suffering. She would rent out a room in her house and would always get these tenants who had anything from small cars to trucks with attached rigs. Regardless of the size, she wouldn't let them park at her house; she would always have them park in front of mine. Her tenants would block my mailbox, and I was constantly getting notices from the postman that I was in jeopardy of not receiving my mail due to the vehicles.

Sunday mornings were supposed to be a day of praise. Yet, there were plenty of those mornings I would back out of my driveway and almost run over the planted rubbish—traps to ruin my spirits. After countless years of dealing with this, I started investigating with other neighbors to figure out how I could prove it was her. I found out they also were getting food (like chicken bones) and other weird things left on their cars and in their mailboxes. They told me the elderly lady I suspected would show up at their front doors in the middle of the night in a stupor.

I prayed to God about how to handle it because I had had quite enough. I told God I really needed His help, as I had reached my wits end. As I was turning the pages of His good book, I could clearly hear Him say to me, "Seek peace first." So I did, and went to her home and rang her doorbell prayed up…really prayed up.

For the very first time, after living near one another for nearly a decade, she answered her door and invited me in. I sat at her dining room table, and we just talked. I shared with her my frustrations as lovingly as I could be considering the circumstance. I was very honest with her about my feelings but tried my best to wrap some love around it. I told her that I had suspected her as the person who had been littering my home. I told her what her tenants had shared with me about her telling them to park at my home and that they said she wouldn't let them park at hers. I also shared with her that I didn't appreciate her telling my mother, upon meeting her, that she'd look after me during those first few encounters, as all I felt she had done was the opposite. She never admitted to doing any of those things, but we left one another in peace and with a commitment to be better neighbors.

Valentine's was a few days away. I wasn't convinced she was ready to love, so I was committed to killing her with kindness. I bought her a Valentine's Day card and wrote her a note and thanked her for our time together and a better future as neighbors. I dropped the note in her mailbox. When she received my card, you would have thought I dropped a million dollars in her bank account. That was the happiest I had ever seen her. It made me realize that this woman was looking for love in the most unusual way. I saw her as a thorn in my side and an enemy, but she was a woman crying for attention with the ugliest of cries.

I had been on such a mission to capture her and punish her for what she was doing to me that I couldn't see past her attacks. I couldn't even see what I was doing to myself. I allowed her to stir my spirit all those years until I sincerely talked to God about it. It wasn't until He knew I was truly ready for the answer that He gave it. "You did not choose me, but I chose you and appointed you to go and bear fruit—fruit that will last. Then the Father will give you whatever you ask in my name. This is my command: Love each other" (John 15:16–17). I had missed it for so long, the remedy…love.

The littering nearly stopped. I think I had only one or two incidents after our talk, but they were so spaced apart that I practically didn't even notice. I never had any more problems after that. I thanked God and would continue to pray for her from time to time...that she'd have a conviction of heart that would cause her to do the reverse of everything she had always known. Eventually, we both moved away, and I don't know what happened to her, but it's a joy to finally know peace.

Love in Action: Loving Your Enemies

1. Pray for your enemies, those who persecute you or seek to use you. With a sincere heart, ask God to give you the remedy.

2. Tell yourself that you won't allow anyone to steal your joy or your peace. It's not worth your energy. You have so many other wonderful things God wants your heart centered on.

3. Shower your enemy with the most amazing love they've ever known. It's not your job to rescue them or be an enabler of bad behavior; that's God's responsibility to save them. It's just your duty to love them.

CHAPTER 25:
LOVING AFTER A LOSS

He will wipe every tear from their eyes. There will be no more death or mourning or crying or pain, for the old order of things has passed away. -Revelation 21:4

RELATIONSHIPS, THEY HELP MAKE US WHO WE ARE. THEY breathe life or death into who we are. Good or bad, they stretch us and grow us into who God intended for us to be. Probably one of the hardest things to do is letting go of someone you love. When you truly love someone, I believe you will always love them. It may not exist with the same level of intensity you once had, but you still love them.

Loss is inevitable. There is not one person who hasn't experienced some kind of loss. Even the greatest household names have stared loss in the eyes in the midst of their journeys. However, the difference between where they are now versus where they could have been was and still is their ability to rise above that loss and see past that moment. His word says, "There is a time for everything, and a season for every activity under the heavens: a time to be born and a time to die, a time to plant and a time to uproot, a time to kill and a time to heal, a time to tear down and a time to build, a time to weep and a time to laugh, a time to mourn and a time to dance" (Ecclesiastes 3:1–4).

Death of a Dream

Dreams give life to our hopes and desires. They allow us to move forward in time and space with an expectation that this hope in us will come to fruition and cause our hearts to smile beyond our wildest conception…that our hope will move from conception to a birthed reality. When you've been dreaming all your life about that singing or acting breakthrough, the birth of your first-born child, being healed from sickness and disease, or even traveling the world, and you come so close that just for a second you hold the dream in hand and then something unexpected happens to ruin it. That six seconds of reality can become fragmenting; it can be devastating; it can be enough to bring you to your knees. But you have to get back up and allow the circumstance to become your teacher of what worked and what didn't work. Enhance what worked and allow yourself to change what didn't work.

Loss of a Relationship

The death of a relationship can be particularly hard when the one left behind is you. When a decision to end a relationship was out of your control and made for you, it can be one of the hardest parts of letting go or seeing any love in your future. You opened yourself at the deepest level you knew how, but he or she still left you. Allowing someone in to find out that their love for you was centered on a selfish provocation for a relationship, or that their position for love was conditional, may not have only been one of your greatest fears but opened a wound that appears incapable of healing. It can be scary to open up to anyone else after such a loss.

You may then find yourself in a never-ending search for closure, but please know there is good reason that door was shut on your behalf. The best you can do for yourself is pray for your healing, forgive the other person(s), learn from any mistakes made, take care of yourself, and not look back. The closure you're seeking could cause further injury while you were hoping for something good. Allow God to do what He knows best. He wants to protect you, so find peace with that and allow Him to provide the reconciliation you both need in His timing and in His way. More than anything, I encourage you to trust His leading and not give up or allow fear to paralyze you and keep you from experiencing real lasting love.

People typically do one of three things after a relational loss: they hop from relationship to relationship wounded, they become runners, or they allow themselves to love again but in a healthier state.

The world would say you need a diversion to get over a relationship, but I've realized that diversions only keep you in an unhealthy state of dead-end relationships. In a diversion, you're not looking at the long-term picture, just the here and now—the immediate fix, the instant gratification. For the serial codependent, they have bought into the lie that another relationship is the answer. They hate the idea of being alone, so when they leave one relationship, they find a new and exciting love with another. They go from relationship to relationship looking for the next high and affix one Band-Aid on top of another. Their hope is that this new love will somehow erase their pain and heal all wounds from their former relationship(s). Such a decision to enter into another relationship is a very emotional one; therefore, it is built on the conditions of what you do. You can identify a serial codependent by their conversation and actions. They are often comparing you with a former relationship and in a hurry to love. They will highlight the things you do well that the other person didn't do but also remind you of things you're not doing that the other person did well. Sometimes you will feel like you can't win for losing, as they are validated against your conversation and actions. Because the love of the serial codependent is conditional, be careful because you will make a mistake; that's just human nature. But the serial codependent will struggle with the disappointments. At the moment you introduce another wound into their lives, they will almost always position themselves for that new and exciting love with another person. That's not your fault. That's just how they know to love. Love them enough not to allow them to play the codependency game with you. They will make mistakes as well, and they wouldn't want you jumping ship at a moment's notice, so let them know your love isn't conditional and show them that in your actions.

Runners are some of the most caring of individuals and have huge hearts. Yet, because the runner has been hurt so badly, they never want to experience the pain of such a loss ever again. You can often find their heads hidden in the sand. They love to hide so you don't see the parts of themselves they fear will cause you to want to leave them behind. Their conversations are often disguised in things like, "I'm never getting married again," "There are no good men out here," or "All women play games." They will often enter into relationships that don't offer commitment because commitment is scary for them. Commitment means opening up to someone again and allowing them to see all of themselves, even their imperfections. If someone offers commitment, they will often self-sabotage or purposely do things to make the other person leave when they don't have the courage to do it themselves. Because the last person hurt them, they will often punish the person in front of them for something that has nothing to do with the current person. With a runner, it's tempting to want to try to save them, but that's not your responsibility. The best way to love them is to see past their desire to run and just be patient and present. Be careful that your loving them is not coming from a place to control or alter their decision to love you back. What they choose to do with your love is their choice; you have no control over whether they will ever run again.

Then there are the healthy connectors, those who take the time and decide to put in the work to be better than their loss. They ask what they can do to improve upon their former decisions or what they can do better for the next relationship versus dwelling on what they did or the other person did wrong. They are owners of their destiny. They look at what they did to contribute to the demise, and they own it. They recognize they are not in control but contributors to where they end up, as they understand the only person who can keep them moving into all that God has for them is them. They trust God enough to know that if He can bring someone into their life so wonderful once, He can do it again and even greater than the last. Healthy connecters look at their circumstances as an abstract versus an absolute; they look for the setup versus the setback. Love never loses its way!

Death of a Loved One

The greater the intensity of the love, the greater the loss. Saying good-bye to someone we love can be heart wrenching. Whether you were there to see them onward to their new life or didn't have a chance to say good-bye, the memory of what once was can be a painful one. You remember all the wonderful times you had with that person and you desire more of that. But life took a turn and made a decision for you that wasn't one you wanted. How, then, do you move forward?

You start with acceptance. You accept they are no longer here in the physical. You accept you will no longer see them again until God calls you to that same place.

You allow yourself to grieve. It's natural to want to hold it together for everyone else, but you also need to allow yourself to respond to your loss that brings you ultimate peace. Stay in prayer. Allow yourself to cry, but be careful that you don't get stuck in grief. Your loved one would want you to experience life fully in their absence.

Allow others to be there for you. There will be people from various aspects of you and your loved one's life to show up for support. They will not always know what to say or do to help ease your pain. Sometimes they may say or do something that goes against what seems commonplace in such matters. For your sanity and well-being, give them the benefit of the doubt that they care about your pain. When asked questions that you just don't have the heart to discuss, you can always respond with, "I'm not in a place to discuss that, but know that I appreciate your love and support during this time." It politely lets them know you don't want to talk about the matter or are not ready to discuss the topic but that you are thankful for their being there for you. It allows you the space to deal with the loss yet room for others to champion you to a new place in your life.

You choose to let them go. Letting them go doesn't mean that you will never experience the pain of the loss. It means you release the ideas and plans you had for their lives as well as any plans you had together. You release them into the hands of the Omnipotent and allow His plans to reign. Romans 8:18 says, "I consider that our present sufferings are not worth comparing with the glory that will be revealed in us." Although you don't understand or know why, you find some way in your heart to trust His decision and know He has a purpose for His choosing to take your loved one.

Honor the memory of your loved one. Honor them by celebrating their life and legacy. Allow their legacy to live on by giving back in some way that would bring tribute to their name and all they stood for. Most importantly, give thanks for the impact they had on your life and those whose lives they touched.

Melton was one who honored the life and legacy of his late wife by choosing to be a light for others. In his thirties, Melton would spend the last four years of his wife's life helping her fight against breast cancer. To watch her go through that process was indescribable for him and their daughter. He had entered into a deep depression after her passing and wasn't sure how he was going to move forward. But the one thing he realized was that no one person could help him regain his strength, only God could. Although he hoped to love again someday, he knew it would be a danger to expect another person to carry all of his heartache and make him feel whole again. As a widowed father, Melton sought the only One he knew could heal and restore his broken heart; he looked to God.

Melton's Story

"Father, help your children, and don't let them fall by the side of the road. And teach them to love one another that Heaven might find a place in their hearts. 'Cause Jesus is love." Those are some of the lyrics from the song "Jesus Is Love" by Lionel Richie and The Commodores. "Jesus Is Love" is my favorite song because of its powerful message.

As a child of God, I am very aware that God is love. 1 John 4:16 (ESV) reads, "God is love, and whoever abides in love abides in God, and God abides in him." We can clearly see that love is God; most importantly, it is tied into our relationship with God. For me, this changed after I lost my first wife to breast cancer. I immediately felt that I would never love again. On that day, March 7, 2010, a part of me died. I died spiritually! Since God is spirit and He is love, then I believe love comes from man's soul. Loving again after you lose someone takes time, but with the help of God, you can love after loss.

Death is man's pathway to the presence of God, but death of a spouse can be a pathway to destruction. When my wife died, I almost instantaneously started putting walls around my heart to stop the pain. Those walls did not stop God from entering my heart; they stopped me from interacting with the world around me. I began to die spiritually, and I fell into a deep depression. I was in a constant fog, and I was not motivated to accomplish anything.

The Dead Sea cannot sustain life because it doesn't let water out. The fresh water of the Jordon River flows in, but the water eventually turns into water saltier than the ocean. The sea has no outlet, so water escapes only by evaporation. Just like the Dead Sea, you will die spiritually if you keep everything inside. God never meant for us to keep everything inside; He commands us to share the good news of the gospel. Revelation 12:11 reads, "They overcame him by the blood of the Lamb and by the word of their testimony; they did not love their lives so much as to shrink from death." What this scripture is simply saying is to apply the Word of God to every situation you face, know your position in Christ, and share your testimony.

Once I began to talk about the passing of my wife and how God sustained me, the walls around my heart began crumbling down. God's love flowed again in my life. I was able to minister to a young man that lost his young girlfriend to breast cancer. My pain and testimony provided him with some comfort during his difficult time. As I found purpose for my pain, God allowed me to meet an exquisite woman who was broken. Her brokenness was the vessel that God used to mend my broken heart. The world sees brokenness or something that's broken as a bad thing, but God sees it as a vessel to heal. God provides comfort to the brokenhearted; look at Psalm 34:18. It reads, "The Lord is close to the brokenhearted and saves those who are crushed in spirit." God took two broken spirits and combined them to make one healthy couple. How can two whole things become one without pieces being removed? God used her to help save my life, and I am forever grateful. She later became my wife, and we have been married now for two years. Love after loss is not an easy road, but with the help of God, you can love again.

Love in Action: Loving After a Loss

1. Spend time in prayer daily, seeking God for strength, healing, and restoration. Allow Him to transform your soul. Live for Him.

2. Allow yourself the ability to grieve your loss. Take care of yourself in the process and allow others to stand with you in your journey to healing.

3. Give tribute to your loss by doing something that brings honor to the memory of a loved one or of a dream deferred. Share your testimony for the good of love.

Chapter 26:
Love Never Fails

For love is as strong as death. -Song of Songs 8:6

LOVE HAS NEVER FAILED; WE HAVE FAILED LOVE. THE good news is that it doesn't have to remain that way. God says you get another chance…seventy times seven, if you need it! As imperfect as we all are and as tough as it can be to love an imperfect person, it is possible to love someone for a lifetime. The only thing keeping you from experiencing this amazing kind of love is you. How you view love will determine how you give and receive it. If you feel like others don't deserve it, it's quite possible that there is some part of you that doesn't believe that you deserve it too. Love is at every corner…just waiting to meet you. If you believe it is there, it will appear.

For Seentahna and Jude, it was truly love at first sight, but a difference in cultures and life would make it difficult for them. They met during a work lunch through a mutual friend. Although finding herself quite smitten by Jude, Seentahna chose to keep her distance because they were business colleagues, but more so because she was Indian and Jude was Filipino. Seentahna was from a very traditional

Indian family, and her culture didn't support nontraditional marriages let alone courtship with other cultures. Yet Jude and Seentahna would continue to cross paths over the next two years through their work friendships. Seentahna, finding herself more and more drawn to Jude, would make it a point to stay away from their mutual circle of friends as to avoid him. It became a standing joke that Jude nicknamed her "MIA" (missing in action). On several occasions, Seentahna would find Jude speaking with her older sister while they were hanging out with friends. As a result, she became even further standoffish, as she thought Jude's interest was with her sister. But Seentahna would soon find out that Jude was inquiring about her through her sister to find out more about who she was. Since Seentahna chose to remain absent, Jude learned of where Seentahna worked out and joined her gym so that he could see her more often. He would send her notes and e-mails. The more his persistence grew, the more she gave him the Heisman. Seentahna's sister thought it wouldn't kill her to at least go on one date with Jude, so she encouraged her. Well, as you can imagine, these two adored one another. The connection was effort-less. It's no surprise that they would enter into an exclusive relation-ship but not without lots of added stresses and strains.

Although her sisters were very aware of their new relationship, Seentahna would spend the next four-plus years keeping Jude hidden from her parents, as she feared being disowned by her family; she thought they would never accept him. This was a struggle for her, as she felt like she was living two different lives. Jude was struggling with being her secret beau, as he was feeling she was ashamed of him. For his love for her was without equal, and he believed love was about following your heart.

During their four-plus years of secrecy, Seentahna would continue to wrestle with the decision to choose to love him or her culture. She would take Jude down this path of an on-again, off-again relationship. She would later make a move from Florida to Atlanta to have some time alone to think about her decision to continue in this relation-ship. Before Jude, Seentahna had gone out with the Indian men of her culture but had never experienced the kind of unconditional love she had with Jude. The men she dated were very much about the man going to work and the woman staying home, but this was far from who she was. She had made up in her mind that she wasn't going to undergo an arranged marriage and would choose who she wanted to marry. After a year of pondering the relationship, Seentahna would move back to Florida. She finally built up the courage to tell her parents about Jude and her love for him. This was by far the scariest thing she had ever done, as it was of the utmost importance to her that her parents accepted him.

Because of her upbringing, she prepared herself for the worst. Just before sharing the news of her love for Jude to her parents, she would pack her bags and load them up in the car in the event they chose to reject her. As she shared, trembling, her love for a man who was the reverse epitome of all her parents had preached to her and her sisters over the years, to her surprise, the complete opposite happened of what she envisioned that meeting would be. Her father, who was a very talkative man, sat in silence. Her mom who was a very quiet woman had tons of questions.

The amazing thing about God is He loves gifting us with His wonder. Although her parents were semiarranged, they still chose to marry one another and at a later time than their culture expected. Seentahna's father knew his daughter well enough to know she had a deep, submissive love and respect for her family and culture yet a strength of courage for her own happiness. He knew she wouldn't come to him with such a heart for a man if she wasn't serious about him. He knew he could choose his culture's tradition and completely cut her out of his life and never see her again, but that wouldn't have been good for either of them. Or he could choose to support what was best for his daughter by continuing to love her and accept her choice of love in her own life. Surprisingly, on that day of dread and fear, with some skepticism of course, her parents made a choice to best support their daughter as much as their hearts could muster.

After taking the courage to share her relationship with her family,

Jude and Seentahna would be separated by miles and countries. Jude was presented with an opportunity to meet some key goals and objectives in his career and seized the opportunity. He took a position in Singapore for about eighteen months and then a transfer to Malaysia for another eighteen months. Although still committed to one another across the miles, this created a lot of frustration in terms of wanting to be together. And when they were able to get together, they dealt with being in each other's space. Jude was trying to make a decision on whether to come back to the United States or permanently remain in Malaysia, so the one thing her father asked of her was to promise him that they would not get engaged without a commitment as to where they would live. Seentahna chose to honor her father's petition, and Jude chose to return to the States. They seamlessly picked up where life had left them.

Later, Seentahna was preparing to attend a cousin's wedding in London, England, and was trying to make a decision about whether to bring Jude with her. As the tradition with the Indian culture was: one, they don't date at all; and two, they don't bring a date to a wedding unless it is their spouse. Because of that, there were many of her family member's spouses that she didn't meet until the day before or at their wedding. So, to say the least, this was a big decision not only for her but for her family. Seentahna's father cautioned her about all the lingering questions she would get about Jude should it not work out between the two of them. He told her he could choose to care about what their society says and not support Jude attending the wedding, or he could support her in him attending the wedding. He told her that, at the end of the day, the choice was hers. After much deliberation, Seentahna told her parents she wanted Jude to attend the wedding with her. When Jude met her family at the London wedding, it was his first time experiencing her culture in its fullness. She explained to her family that they weren't married nor engaged, so when her cousin responded with "You're here! It's a done deal!" and embraced him as family, it was at that moment that Jude finally got what Seentahna was wrestling with all those years and the magnitude of her introducing him to her family. Seentahna got to watch God change the hearts of her parents and now her family.

During the wedding festivities, Jude and Seentahna found a couple of days in the schedule to steal away to Paris. They had always wanted to visit Pont des Arts—the Paris bridge of love locks, the bridge where lovers lock their eternal love and devotion for one another. Jude would find a place to buy a lock and secretly attach the ring he had planned for Seentahna to the lock. As they were having breakfast at Café Lateral, Jude suggested they go put their lock on the bridge that day. When Seentahna asked him if he brought the lock, he replied, "Yes, but I need you to help me write it…or finish writing it." As he pulled out the lock with the ring on it, she could see he had prewritten on the lock the words "Will you marry me?" Seentahna replied, "Are you serious!" Jude replied, "Uh, do you see the ring? Of course I'm serious!" With a heart overflowing with so much love and tears of joy, Seentahna said, "YES!" and proceeded to write "Yes" on the other side of the lock. After all the hardship and family challenges, they had learned how to hold on to each other and now had a love that was as strong as death. They were committed to accomplishing life together forever and supporting one another in their respective dreams. After they had taken in the moment, they made their way to the bridge and secured their lock on the bridge. They tossed their key in the Seine River, signifying their forever devotion.

After their return from Paris, they met up with her cousins at a venue. This would turn out to be a semiengagement party. Seentahna had never had a chance to share any big life moments with her cousins in London, so although it was a semi-impromptu proposal for Jude, the moment couldn't have been more perfect.

Jude and Seentahna have since completed premarital counseling through the Catholic faith and are preparing for a big Hindu wedding as I write. One of the things that Seentahna shared while they were in premarital counseling is that they each had to volunteer to share their own story. She said that as she listened, there were so many stories where people had broken up and found their way back to one another over time and distance that it was a joy to hear. Seentahna and Jude have endeavored nine years of preparedness. More than anything, they are now ready to spend the rest of their lives as one until death do them part. I couldn't be happier for them! To Seentahna and Jude and to love that never fails!

Love in Action: Love Never Fails (Winning in Love)

1. Write a prayer of thanks for the love God's gifted you. Even if the love you desire has yet to arrive, thank God in advance, trust, and believe! "If you believe, you will receive whatever you ask for in prayer" (Matthew 21:22).

2. Don't overthink it. Allow love to have its place in your life. Sit back and enjoy the ride!

3. Do something special for your love that shows him or her you love them without condition and for eternity. Enjoy the loving!

MY STORY 2.0

MY STORY 2.0

You have the power to say this is not
how the story ends. -Unknown

THOUGHT LOVE HAD TAKEN ME OUT. I DIDN'T KNOW
how long I was going to be in that somber place, but I knew I
wanted out. I also wanted out of the same old cycles. I'd always been
someone who had done things with excellence, but that area of my
life just hadn't been that. I could have settled by now, but I'd waited
this long...I wanted extraordinary. And I know my God can do the
impossible.

It took many months for me to come to a place of peace and
understanding. Ironically, what seemed like one of the most painful
seasons of my life had turned out to be one of my greatest teachers
and has been my best adventure thus far. I'm watching God transform
me into a woman I hardly recognize. I like the new me much better
than the old me. In the midst of it all, I have gained a real perspective
of what true love is. I've learned to have a healthy sense of self-love. I
no longer allow the expectations and pressures of others about marriage and children to define my worth, and I stopped doing that to

myself too. In my past relationships, I was looking to satisfy things in my life that only God could fulfill. With all of the unanswered questions as to why I wasn't married with a family of my own, I chose to let go. Regardless of how things ended, I chose to forgive and pray for those who hurt me along the way. And I forgave myself for inflicting that same hurt to myself. In spite of everything, I've chosen to love.

Those dark days are now filled with this amazing, unimaginable kind of love. God's angels were around me all along. I was just too busy to notice them. I was too focused on what I wanted and believed I didn't have. Now, I see His angels everywhere. At every turn, they're smiling at me, which makes me smile back. On the elevator, it's like they're waiting to make my day…like they're cheering me on to somewhere that I have no idea as to where. But this time, I'm not focused on the destination. I don't care because I'm enjoying the ride. I find myself grinning like a woman smitten by love. And it's because I am. It's different, though…different than how I imagined love would be. I'm in love with life and all that it has to offer. I finally know what I want and not just a list of what I don't want. I choose to live and not dwell in the deepest of the dark. The peace that He's given me is immeasurable. I was looking for it in one person, but God chose to multiply that love in many. He's sent those who have helped me change my conversation, those who won't let me not hope or think anything but what's for my good and the good of others. He's surrounded me with people who choose to see the value in me and others and who cherish their relationships. I can remember so many nights and days praying to God, "Use me, Lord. Use me for your Honor and Glory." Now, that I'm having the time of my life, I want Him to use me some more.

What I didn't expect was that you would be reading this book. Several years ago, I felt God leading me to be a mouthpiece for love and relationships…more specifically a catalyst of change for healthy relationships based on God's guidelines and principles. I never saw myself being in the forefront, so I wasn't sure what exactly that leading was going to look like or when it would take place. I assumed that it would be after I was married with kids and gained a "certain perspective" that I felt could render advice on love and relationships. I figured it would be after the business had reached certain heights that I would be entertaining this feat. I would journal from time to time, after I felt His leading me to be a facilitator for change, about certain events and relationships that would take place in my life but just kept everything stashed away. But a little over a year ago, God was saying the time was now. It was March 2014, to be exact, that I felt God leading me to write a book on the topic of love. The title of the book had come to mind, but honestly I just sat on it. It wasn't until two months later that I began journaling about the topic. As I started writing *Love: The Greatest Gift*, I found writings from several years ago where God was preparing me for such a time as this. The things I had experienced in my relationships weren't about me at all. It was about bringing healing to the many of those whose stories resemble mine and those stories shared in the aforementioned pages. It was all about His ultimate plan and the positioning of each of our futures. It was about the greatest gift: love…His love.

During that last lag of my thirty-ninth year, little did I know that I would be introduced to the wise servant I previously mentioned who would share with me the story about the eagle stirring the nest. Our conversation centered on me moving from Dallas to Houston to establish a new future. We discussed God's leading to make us uncomfortable to prepare us for the next step. I had some prior discomfort about the idea of leaving Dallas. I have never imagined myself being anywhere but Dallas, and I certainly had not imagined myself in Houston. I wasn't sure why, although I had concocted good reasons in my head as to what made sense at the time. I told my wise friend I would certainly pray about it. I had spent my entire adult life (post-college) in Dallas. The truth of the matter is that I had gotten stuck and complacent there. When I stayed in Dallas, the pain kept harassing me. My home that I had lived in for so many years and had served as a source of great refuge and peace was now a constant reminder of discomfort.

Several months later, I would be invited to have dinner with a gentleman I had just met a week prior. The date was okay; it seemed like we were straining to find something to talk about. Toward the end of the evening, I asked him where he attended church. Suddenly, he seemed relaxed and began to share his experiences about seminary, and I found myself intrigued. As he spoke, he began, for some reason, to share with me the story of Jonah. I knew the story but don't think I REALLY knew the story in full. As he shared the infamous adventure of the man in the belly of the great fish, he mentioned the name of my book in the midst of his conversation. I didn't understand the correlation. For at this point, I hadn't shared with anyone the name of my book, nor do I remember telling anyone that I was considering writing a book. The fact that he mentioned the story of Jonah around the name of this book made it my mission to go home and read the story in its entirety.

Interestingly enough, God had given Jonah an assignment to go to the great city of Ninevah to share the message of salvation to those who were considered wicked. Jonah didn't like—well, actually hated—the Assyrians, so he decided he wasn't going to fulfill the assignment and instead headed in the opposite direction to Tarshish. He found a ship in Joppa bound for sea. When Jonah got on the ship, a great wind arose and caused a violent storm that threatened the lives of all on board. When the sailors concluded that Jonah was the cause of the storm, they prayerfully tossed Jonah from the ship to calm the sea. There Jonah found himself in the belly of this great fish for three days and three nights. During this time, he prayed to God for help and said he would fulfill his vow to spread God's message. It was at Jonah's commitment to serve that God rescued him from the fish. Jonah then went to Ninevah and shared God's message of salvation for all. They repented and believed and were saved. Great story, but I still didn't get it at the time.

A month later, I would attend a mini conference in Houston for work. As I learned about the many opportunities Houston had to offer for my consulting practice, I thought it would be great to expand into the Houston market. So I made plans to expand my business there, but I was set on staying in Dallas while doing so. I was traveling back and forth to certification training and different business events. At every encounter, someone was asking about my moving or telling me I would be moving to Houston. I wanted to make it clear that I was staying in Dallas but expanding my business into the Houston market, but the inquiries and the nudges kept coming. The funny thing is that every person that was asking about or prophesying a move to Houston was unaware of the former prompting.

In September, I was attending a meeting with one of the local organizations and the chair introduced me as someone who had just moved to Houston. Everyone was so warm and welcoming. For whatever reason that day, I didn't correct her or take a stance on Dallas over Houston. As I left the meeting, something was rousing in me about a move to Houston. I shared my thoughts with a friend of mine about this stirring, and we discussed scenarios about how this could possibly play out. As I drove back to Dallas that next day, I relented and told God that if He wanted me to move to Houston, I was there. I wasn't going to fight Him anymore on my plans over His. By the time I arrived in Dallas, there was something telling me that my stint in Dallas was over. There was a peace about this next chapter.

In October, I packed up the many years of memories and sentiments and prepared for this new road ahead. The night of my going-away social, I shared with a friend about my plans to write a book and how I was letting go of needing to do things my way. For years prior to my move to Houston, I would watch Joel Osteen just about every Sunday before heading to church to hear my pastor, Bryan Carter, preach. I had never attended Lakewood Church on a Sunday until I moved to Houston. The first Sunday I visited Lakewood, Pastor Joel preached "Choosing Faith in Spite of the Facts" from one of my favorite scriptures, Proverbs 3:5–6. The following Sunday, the sermon was entitled "Covered by Mercy," in which Pastor Joel told the story of Jonah (how fitting). It was confirmation that I was where I was supposed to be. A few weeks later, that same friend who I'd shared my plans with to write a book would connect me with my future coauthor of my first book, *Shift: Twenty Women Share Stories of Strength, Courage, and Succeeding Against the Odds.*

As I was entering this new season of my life, the scales of the old one began to fall off. Pastor Joel would later preach on eagles, and my path would cross with several others who also shared with me stories on the flight of an eagle. God had taken me back over my journey, from my encounter with the wise man, to the date that had me running home to read about this man named Jonah, and all the myriad of promptings to a move to the great city of Houston. It was in that year of review that I realized it was all by His design. Once again, He was setting me up for this amazing blessing—more than my heart could hold—and I almost missed it. My cup was running over, and my heart was beginning to mend.

This is the most healthy my heart has been in a very long time, and I can't tell you how wonderful that feels. The tears I shed now are filled with more joy because I can't believe how God could transform such a dark season of my life and make it brand new. Although not yet married with children, my life no longer feels empty or broken. It feels whole. I still have my old, long-standing, rich friendships, yet God has filled my life with some new ones and this new, unimaginable love. Through these wonderful relationships, God has shown me what real love looks like, so I can only hope the best is yet to come. When I finally stopped to smell the roses, I could see that all around me was love. There was more laughter and more smiles. There were those who weren't afraid to say, "Hey, you're good, but this is how you can be better, and I'm going to stay by your side until you get there." The love is endless, and I am overwhelmed by His goodness. I am learning to really love myself, and it feels freeing to say no when I need to do so. I can't say that I've arrived, as I feel like it's a process, but I can say I've come to know love like no other. Although I miss my family and friends back in the D, I love my new city. Every day is a new adventure. I feel alive and ready.

The message God wants to convey is for each of us to know and understand His love is available to all, no matter where you've been or how bad you feel you've messed up. There is absolutely nothing you can do that can ever separate you from His love. He can love you no less than His greatest love for you. He doesn't love with the conditions that we so often do. He says that His love is unconditional, and He's challenging us all to love as He does. It's yours for the asking, and He gives it freely. All you have to do is unwrap the gift!

RESOURCES

Chapter 18: Loving Through Courtship

- *Choosing God's Best: Wisdom for Lifelong Romance* by Dr. Don Raunikar

- *Lies at the Altar: The Truth About Great Marriages* by Dr. Robin L. Smith

- *Temptations of the Single Girl: The Ten Dating Traps You Must Avoid* by Nina Atwood

- *The Five Love Languages: How to Express Heartfelt Commitment to Your Mate* by Gary Chapman

Chapter 19: Loving Your Spouse

- *The Power of a Praying Wife* and *The Power of a Praying Husband* by Stormie Omartian

Chapter 21: Loving Your Blended Family

- *The Smart Stepfamily Marriage: Keys to Success in the Blended Family* and *The Smart Stepfamily: Seven Steps to a Healthy Family* by Ron L. Deal

ABOUT THE AUTHOR

BESTSELLING AUTHOR, SPEAKER, AND BUSINESSWOMAN, Jacqueline Camphor is the Founder and Managing Director of Accentuals Consulting LLC, a company specializing in services ranging from business process design to accounting system implementations. Jacqueline enjoys coaching others to financial health and has helped numerous clients reach their financial goals, including budgeting, savings, and debt freedom. In 2014, she accepted the call to spread the message about loving unconditionally in relationships and is fast becoming known as the *Love and Money* consultant.

Jacqueline is co-author of the bestselling book, *Shift: Twenty Women Share Stories of Strength, Courage, and Succeeding Against the Odds*, presented by Nikki Woods (global visibility expert and senior producer of the Tom Joyner Morning Show).

A dedicated community advocate, Jacqueline is passionate about giving back. She is a runner, culinarian, and cosmopolitan traveler who follows her own motto, "You only get one life, so live it!"

Jacqueline currently resides in Houston, Texas.

Contact Information

Accentuals Consulting, LLC
1700 Post Oak Boulevard, Suite 600
Houston, TX 77056
(832) 586-8333

Visit www.jacquelinecamphor.com to inquire about speaking engagements.

You may also follow her on:
Twitter @jacquiecamphor or
Facebook.com/jacqueline.camphor

56308686R00128

Made in the USA
Charleston, SC
15 May 2016